PLACE IN RETURN BOX to remove this checkout from your record
TO AVOID FINES return on or before date due.

DATE DUE	DATE DUE	DATE DUE
JAN 5 1993		
213		

MSU Is An Affirmative Action/Equal Opportunity Institution

D1349179

TINKER GUIDE TO
LATIN AMERICAN AND CARIBBEAN
POLICY AND SCHOLARLY
RESOURCES
IN METROPOLITAN NEW YORK

Edited by

RONALD G. HELLMAN
& BETH KEMPLER PFANNL

BILDNER CENTER
FOR WESTERN HEMISPHERE STUDIES

The Graduate School and University Center
The City University of New York

Library of Congress Cataloging-in-Publication Data

Tinker guide to Latin American and Caribbean policy and scholarly resources in
    metropolitan New York / edited by Ronald G. Hellman & Beth Kempler Pfannl. --
    1st ed.
      p.   cm.
    Includes indexes.
    1. Latin America--Study and teaching--New York Metropolitan Area--
Directories. 2. West Indies--Study and teaching--New York Metropolitan Area--
Directories. 3. Latin America--Library resources--New York Metropolitan Area--
Directories. 4. West Indies--Library resources--New York Metropolitan Area--
Directories. 5. Latin America--Archival resources--New York Metropolitan Area--
Directores. 6. West Indies--Archival resources--New York Metropolitan Area--
Directories. I. Hellman, Ronald G. II. Pfannl, Beth Kempler.
F1409.95.U6T56 1988
972.9'0025'7471--dc19   88-8186
ISBN 0-929972-00-7
ISBN 0-929972-01-5 (pbk.)

Cover:
Original photo by Loren Ellis
Cover design by André Boucher

Manufactured in the United States of America
First Edition

CONTENTS

INTRODUCTION

New York City is the nation's hub for Latin American and Caribbean affairs in commerce, finance, international diplomacy, communications and education. Until now, however, a comprehensive guide to New York's Latin American and Caribbean resources in the area of public policy, international relations and the social sciences has not existed.

In response to the increasing interest in this area of the world and the need for such a guide, the Bildner Center for Western Hemisphere Studies prepared, and is pleased to publish, the *Tinker Guide to Latin American and Caribbean Policy and Scholarly Resources in Metropolitan New York.*

The project was funded with grants from The Tinker Foundation Incorporated. The Foundation is concerned with activities related to Ibero-America, Spain and Portugal within the broad field of the social sciences, with particular emphasis in areas such as international relations, urban and regional studies, education, communications management and economics. The Tinker Foundation also encourages natural resource development projects, training of specialists at the post-graduate level and programs designed to further the education of Spanish- and Portuguese-speaking people of the United States.

The Bildner Center is part of The Graduate School and University Center of The City University of New York (CUNY), and sponsors research, forums, seminars and publications that address the practical resolution of public policy problems facing the nations of the Western Hemisphere. The Center coordinates related scholarly interests of the faculties of CUNY's eighteen senior and community colleges, and encourages the full use of their resources in the study of Latin American public policy concerns. The Bildner Center serves as a link between the City University's community of scholars and other experts and practitioners working on contemporary issues in Latin America, North America and the Caribbean. The Center is named for Albert Bildner in recognition of his efforts and contributions in establishing the Center, and his continuing support.

The *Tinker Guide* is a unique compilation of organizations and collections in the New York area that constitute sources of information and assistance to scholars, business persons, students and others interested in scholarly and policy related issues. It does not include the vast number of cultural and artistic institutions in the area with collections and activities related to Latin America and the Caribbean.

The *Tinker Guide* contains sections, with entries arranged in alphabetical order, on academic institutions; associations, nonprofit organizations and research centers; chambers of commerce and government offices; United Nations agencies; Latin American and Caribbean consulates and missions; and libraries. Each entry is numbered and gives the name, address and telephone number of the organization, and describes its Latin American and Caribbean-related activities and collections. This information was obtained from questionnaires completed for this project by each organization, as well as through interviews. Appended, additionally, are listings of bookstores and publishing houses, the media, and the *Tinker Guide to City University of New York Scholars of Latin American and Caribbean Affairs*. Finally, two general indices, one by name and the other by subject, which refer to the number assigned to each entry, facilitate the retrieval of the information.

The cooperation, assistance and support of numerous individuals made this project possible. We extend foremost our gratitude to Martha Twitchell Muse, Chairman and President of The Tinker Foundation, for her support. We are grateful to all the members of the institutions contacted for inclusion in this Guide who cooperated and contributed their time and attention to complete our questionnaire and respond to our enquiries and to Mitsui and Company (U.S.A.), Inc., for its initial contribution in support of this guide. Moreover, we wish to express our appreciation to the very able staff of the Bildner Center for their assistance. Special thanks must be extended to Saphira Baker and Melissa Hyams for their thorough research during the initial phase of the project; to André Boucher for the diligent and impeccable computer processing; to Diego Fragueiro, who attended most efficiently to all aspects of the concluding phase, including final research, collection, processing and editing; and to Sheila Klee, Managing Editor, Bildner Center publications, for her useful advice throughout the duration of the project.

We welcome any additions and suggestions for future editions.

ACADEMIC
INSTITUTIONS

The following information was requested for each entry in this section. However, final entries contain only those categories which each organization deemed applicable.

Identification:
- Name
- Address
- Telephone

Affiliation

Degrees and subjects offered

Program activities

Library and research facilities

ADELPHI UNIVERSITY
Latin American Studies Program
South Avenue
Garden City, NY 11530
(516) 294-8700 Ext. 7434

DEGREES AND SUBJECTS OFFERED
B.A.; anthropology, history, economics, languages (Portuguese and Spanish required), political science and sociology.

PROGRAM ACTIVITIES
Monthly lectures (e.g., Press Freedom in Latin America); topical forums (e.g., Dominican Republic elections); films.

LIBRARY/RESEARCH FACILITIES
Excellent Spanish-language holdings in contemporary literature; computerized cataloguing system; ERIC.

BERNARD M. BARUCH COLLEGE
OF THE CITY UNIVERSITY OF NEW YORK
Department of Black and Hispanic Studies
17 Lexington Avenue
New York, NY 10010
(212) 505-5973

AFFILIATION
The City University of New York.

DEGREES AND SUBJECTS OFFERED
A minor is offered in Black and Hispanic Studies. Apart from a course in Latin American institutions and culture, most courses deal with Puerto Rico. Topics treated in the courses cover Puerto Rican historical, social, political, and economic development; contemporary Puerto Rican society, and specific social issues related to Puerto Ricans, both in Puerto Rico and in the U.S.

PROGRAM ACTIVITIES
Regular lectures and open forums are held. Hispanic Celebration Week and Puerto Rico Discovery Day celebrations take place in Spring and Fall, respectively.

LIBRARY/RESEARCH FACILITIES
A collection of material, both in English and Spanish, is maintained.

BROOKLYN COLLEGE
OF THE CITY UNIVERSITY OF NEW YORK
Africana Studies
Bedford Avenue & Avenue H
Brooklyn, NY 11210
(718) 780-5597/5598

AFFILIATION
The City University of New York.

DEGREES AND SUBJECTS OFFERED
The B.A. degree program in Africana Studies requires 27 credits plus any prerequisite of the courses from the groups of the Africana Studies Department. Courses related to Latin America and the Caribbean deal with topics such as the slave trade and its impact, the experiences of Africans in the New World, African religion and culture in the New World, Caribbean cultures and political systems.

Graduate courses on the political economy of the Caribbean and summer seminars on this area are also offered.

PROGRAM ACTIVITIES
The Humanities Institute at Brooklyn College frequently offers programs on the Caribbean area.

LIBRARY/RESEARCH FACILITIES
The Brooklyn College Library has good research facilities for undergraduate programs.

BROOKLYN COLLEGE
OF THE CITY UNIVERSITY OF NEW YORK
Area Studies
Bedford Avenue & Avenue H
Brooklyn, NY 11210
(718) 780-5451

AFFILIATION
The City University of New York.

DEGREES AND SUBJECTS OFFERED
A B.A. with a major in Latin American Area Studies requires a minimum of 24 cred-

its of courses approved by the coordinator plus at least two semesters of Spanish or Portuguese. Twelve of the 24 credits must be concentrated in one department and the other 12 must be chosen from at least three other departments. The participating departments are Africana Studies, Anthropology and Archæology, Comparative Literature, Economics, History, Political Science, Portuguese, Puerto Rican Studies and Spanish.

PROGRAM ACTIVITIES
The Humanities Institute at Brooklyn College frequently sponsors programs relating to the Latin American area.

LIBRARY/RESEARCH FACILITIES
The Brooklyn College Library has good research facilities for undergraduate programs.

**BROOKLYN COLLEGE
OF THE CITY UNIVERSITY OF NEW YORK
Caribbean Studies**
*Bedford Avenue &Avenue H
Brooklyn, NY 11210
(718) 780-5350/5597*

AFFILIATION
The City University of New York.

DEGREES AND SUBJECTS OFFERED
The B.A. degree in Caribbean Studies requires a double major: a major in any department of the college plus 18 credits of approved courses in the departments of Africana Studies, French, History, Political Science, Puerto Rican Studies and Spanish. These courses may include up to six credits in relevant special topics courses and/or seminars.

PROGRAM ACTIVITIES
The Humanities Institute at Brooklyn College frequently offers programs on the Caribbean area.

LIBRARY/RESEARCH FACILITIES
The Brooklyn College Library has good research facilities for undergraduate programs.

**BROOKLYN COLLEGE
OF THE CITY UNIVERSITY OF NEW YORK
Puerto Rican Studies**
*Bedford Avenue & Avenue H
Brooklyn, NY 11210
(718) 780-5561/5563*

AFFILIATION
The City University of New York.

DEGREES AND SUBJECTS OFFERED
The B.A. degree program in Puerto Rican Studies requires 27-33 credits plus 18 credits in courses from another department chosen in consultation with a department counselor. Graduate courses such as Puerto Rican Society, Puerto Rican Communities in Urban Areas and Bilingualism: Characteristics and Practices are also offered for students in other fields.

PROGRAM ACTIVITIES
The Humanities Institute at Brooklyn College frequently offers programs on the Caribbean area.

LIBRARY/RESEARCH FACILITIES
The Brooklyn College Library has good research facilities for undergraduate programs.

**THE CITY COLLEGE
OF THE CITY UNIVERSITY OF NEW YORK
Department of Latin American
and Hispanic Caribbean Studies**
*138th Street at Convent Avenue
New York, NY 10031
(212) 690-6763*

AFFILIATION
The City University of New York.

DEGREES AND SUBJECTS OFFERED
B.A. degrees: Latin American Area Studies; Puerto Rican Studies. Interdisciplinary courses on Latin America, Puerto Rico, the Hispanic Caribbean and Studies of Hispanics in the United States.

PROGRAM ACTIVITIES
Conferences, seminars, forums and special lectures are given on an irregular but more or less continuous basis.

LIBRARY/RESEARCH FACILITIES
The Department has a reading room which contains published materials on Latin America, the Caribbean and Hispanics in the United States.

COLUMBIA UNIVERSITY
Center for the Study of Human Rights
International Affairs Building, Room 704
Columbia University, 420 West 118th Street
New York,NY 10027
(212) 280-2479

AFFILIATION
Columbia University.

DEGREES AND SUBJECTS OFFERED
The Center sponsors interdisciplinary graduate and undergraduate courses and seminars on human rights. It does not offer a degree program. Students and others interested in research on human rights will find that existing degree programs at the university can usually be adapted to their requirements. In cooperation with faculty members at Columbia and other universities, the Center prepares introductory and advanced-level courses on human rights. A series of published syllabi provides sample courses on different aspects of human rights, each including topical bibliographies.

PROGRAM ACTIVITIES
The Center hosts several conferences per year on current issues and trends in human rights. The Whitney M. Young Jr. Distinguished Lecture on race relations brings a distinguished person to Columbia for a few days each year for lecture and discussion. Programs include: year-long residencies for postdoctoral research; an annual international symposium held in June for teachers and researchers from the U.S. and abroad; monthly discussions of research papers by a group of scholars and other human rights specialists; and medical seminars on ethics, rights and medicine.

LIBRARY/RESEARCH FACILITIES
The Center maintains a small collection of basic human rights books and United Nations Committee documents and uses the Columbia University library system.

COLUMBIA UNIVERSITY
The Institute of Latin American
and Iberian Studies
International Affairs Building, 8th Floor
420 West 118th Street
New York, NY 10027
(212) 280-4643/5468

AFFILIATION
Columbia University.

DEGREES AND SUBJECTS OFFERED
Courses available include anthropology, art history, business, economics, geography, history, health sciences, literature/comparative literature, political science, Spanish conversation and composition, Portuguese language and composition as well as Latin American literature. Certificates are available at the B.A., M.A. and Ph.D. levels; no degrees are offered.

PROGRAM ACTIVITIES
Tutorials are available in Aymara and Quechua. The summer training program funded by The Tinker Foundation provides funds for transportation and maintenance for summer research overseas. For student support, NDEA Title VI Fellowships are available for tuition. Departmental Research Assistantships and Chase Manhattan Bank Fellowships are also granted. Reed Summer Fellowships are available for research.

A speaker series on international finance and trade is offered as well as university seminars on Latin America.

LIBRARY/RESEARCH FACILITIES
The Columbia Libraries contain an extensive collection of volumes, periodical titles and newspaper subscriptions on Latin America and the Caribbean.

EMPIRE STATE COLLEGE
OF THE STATE UNIVERSITY OF NEW YORK
Metropolitan New York Regional Center
Bilingual Program
107 Suffolk Street
New York, NY 10002
(212) 598-0672

AFFILIATION
The State University of New York.

DEGREES AND SUBJECTS OFFERED
B.A. and M.A. in Cultural Studies, including Caribbean and Latin American Studies, Spanish Language and Linguistics.

PROGRAM ACTIVITIES
Study groups (seminars), Program of Distant Learning and Individualized Learning.

LIBRARY/RESEARCH FACILITIES
Limited collection of books distributed in different units. Extensive collection of Latin American photography.

FORDHAM UNIVERSITY
Puerto Rican Studies Institute
113 West 60th Street
New York, NY 10023
(212) 841-5266

AFFILIATION
Fordham University, Lincoln Center Campus.

DEGREES AND SUBJECTS OFFERED
B.A. Degree is offered in Puerto Rican Studies major and minor and Bilingual-Bicultural Studies major and minor. An interdisciplinary approach is followed in the study of Puerto Rico and the rest of the Caribbean, Central and South America. The Institute also offers courses dealing with the social, economic, political and cultural situation of Puerto Ricans and other Hispanics in the U.S.

PROGRAM ACTIVITIES
The Institute periodically sponsors conferences and seminars dealing with subjects related to Latin America and Hispanics in the U.S., as well as cultural and artistic events, such as concerts and exhibitions.

THE GRADUATE SCHOOL
AND UNIVERSITY CENTER
OF THE CITY UNIVERSITY OF NEW YORK
Bildner Center for Western Hemisphere Studies
33 West 42nd Street
New York, NY 10036
(212) 382-2047

AFFILIATION
The Graduate School and University Center of the City University of New York.

DEGREES AND SUBJECTS OFFERED
The Center does not offer degrees or courses; however it serves as an advisor to students and faculty throughout the CUNY system on topics related to research on Latin America and the Caribbean. Internships for academic credit are offered by special arrangement.

PROGRAM ACTIVITIES
The Center sponsors several major public forums, conferences, seminars and roundtable discussions yearly. Recent topics have included: *Confronting Revolution: Security Through Diplomacy in Central America; New York-Buenos Aires: Issues in Urban Housing and Health; International Symposium on the Problems of Contemporary Democracy in Chile; The Democratic Challenge in Peru; The Urban Challenge in Mexico City; Argentina: The Struggle for Democracy.* The Center has a continuing series of programs and research on contemporary Mexico.

LIBRARY/RESEARCH FACILITIES
The Center maintains a specialized library of newsletters and current Latin American & Caribbean periodicals. These reference materials may be used in the Center's offices.

The Center's own publications include policy paper series on *Changing Global Political Economy and U.S.-Latin American Relations* and *the Urban Challenge in the Western Hemisphere* as well as a number of *Discussion Excerpts* and Working Papers. These may be borrowed or purchased.

**THE GRADUATE SCHOOL
AND UNIVERSITY CENTER
OF THE CITY UNIVERSITY OF NEW YORK
Research Group on Socialism and Democracy**
*33 West 42nd Street
New York, NY 10036
(212) 642-2401*

AFFILIATION
The City University of New York. A project of the Ph.D. Program in Sociology of the Graduate School and University Center of the City University of New York.

PROGRAM ACTIVITIES
Fields of research include politics and culture in Latin America; repression and resistance to violence in South and Central America; socialist movements and parties in Latin America; problems of social and socialist development in countries undergoing rapid change and faced with U.S. hostility. Thus far, the Group has

sponsored the following lectures and discussions concerned with South and Central America: James Petras on the problems of transition to socialism in Latin America; Susanne Jonas on the Sandinista movement and problem of socialist construction in small Third World countries; Jean Franco on "Death Camp Confessions and Resistance to Violence in Latin America."

LIBRARY/RESEARCH FACILITIES
The Group is in touch with study groups and research centers in many parts of the world. Some of these groups send their materials and publications. Contact has been established with scholars in several Central American and Caribbean countries.

THE HISPANIC INSTITUTE OF THE UNITED STATES
612 West 116th Street
New York, NY 10027
(212) 280-4187

14

AFFILIATION
Spanish and Portuguese Department of Columbia University.

PROGRAM ACTIVITIES
Conferences and concerts are organized.

LIBRARY/RESEARCH FACILITIES
The Institute maintains outstanding archives and collections of literature and folklore in Spanish and Portuguese.

EUGENIO MARIA DE HOSTOS COMMUNITY COLLEGE OF THE CITY UNIVERSITY OF NEW YORK
Latin American and Caribbean Studies
500 Grand Concourse
Bronx, NY 10451
(212) 960-1075

15

AFFILIATION
The City University of New York.

DEGREES AND SUBJECTS OFFERED
Hostos Community College offers a two-semester Latin American History course, and courses dealing mostly with Puerto Rico and the Caribbean, including such

topics as literature, history and a variety of courses on social and cultural issues. Students may graduate with a concentration in Latin American and Caribbean Studies.

PROGRAM ACTIVITIES
Occasional lectures are organized with the coordination of student clubs. Film showings are also organized.

LIBRARY/RESEARCH FACILITIES
A collection of material, in both English and Spanish, is maintained, including books, periodicals, and a variety of audiovisual resources.

**HUNTER COLLEGE
OF THE CITY UNIVERSITY OF NEW YORK
Center for Puerto Rican Studies**
*695 Park Avenue, Box 548
New York, NY 10021
(212) 772-5689
(212) 772-4197 (Library)*

AFFILIATION
The City University of New York.

PROGRAM ACTIVITIES
The Center's research activities focus on Puerto Rican society and the links between the homeland and its extensions in the U.S., including studies of culture, political economy of migration, speech and ways of speaking, intergenerational perspectives on bilingualism, Puerto Ricans in higher education, and the Puerto Rican labor movement. Research results are published in working papers, journals and books. Offers summer seminars and participates in conferences and organizations concerned with Puerto Rican welfare.

LIBRARY/RESEARCH FACILITIES
The Center maintains a library of 6,000 volumes, books, dissertations, documents, periodicals and films on Puerto Rican history, culture, language and education. In 1984, the Center joined with Mexican American Studies centers at Stanford University, the University of California at Los Angeles and the University of Texas at Austin to constitute the Inter-University Project (IUP) on Latino Research. IUP has been funded to carry out research on Latino populations on a national scale, to administer a major research competition on social policy for these communities and to promote the development of researchers and scholarship on issues of importance to Latino peoples.

HUNTER COLLEGE
OF THE CITY UNIVERSITY OF NEW YORK
Latin American and Caribbean Studies Program
695 Park Avenue
New York, NY 10021
(212) 772-4285/4286

AFFILIATION
The City University of New York.

DEGREES AND SUBJECTS OFFERED
The inter-disciplinary area specialization in Latin American and Carribean Studies consisting of 36 credits leads to a B.A. degree. The courses form a combined major/minor, with 24 core credits dealing with the Latin American and Caribbean areas, plus a 12-credit minor. The core courses are drawn from the Divisions of Social Sciences, Humanities and the Arts. Students select courses for the major and minor components in consultation with the program's director.

PROGRAM ACTIVITIES
Each year, students participate in the Model OAS in Washington, D.C. Over the course of an academic year, the program sponsors and co-sponsors symposia, lectures, films and other events designed to focus discussion on issues in the Americas.

LIBRARY/RESEARCH FACILITIES
The Hunter College Library has an extensive number of books on Latin America and the Caribbean.

HERBERT H. LEHMAN COLLEGE
OF THE CITY UNIVERSITY OF NEW YORK
Latin American and Caribbean Studies
Bedford Park Boulevard West
Bronx, NY 10468
(212) 960-4999

AFFILIATION
The City University of New York.

DEGREES AND SUBJECTS OFFERED
B.A. in Latin American and Caribbean Studies consists of a regular major and designated courses in Latin American and Caribbean studies. The program started in January 1985.

PROGRAM ACTIVITIES
Film series on Latin America.

LIBRARY/RESEARCH FACILITIES
A collection of relevant subject material is maintained.

MARYMOUNT MANHATTAN COLLEGE
Department of Modern Languages
221 East 71st Street
New York, NY 10021
(212) 517-0606/0507

DEGREES AND SUBJECTS OFFERED
B.A. in Spanish with tracks in Spanish and international affairs, business manage-
ment, or Double Language Major; B.A. in International Affairs with specialization in
Latin America. Courses offered in all of the above fields.

PROGRAM ACTIVITIES
Sponsors lectures, performance-demonstration programs, forums on public policy and conferences with other organizations dealing with the Hispanic world or
with Hispanic culture. Movie series, guided visits to events of Hispanic interest in
New York City, and travel/study to the Hispanic world are also available.

LIBRARY/RESEARCH FACILITIES
The Thomas J. Shanahan Library has holdings in Spanish and Latin American
studies as well as in international affairs. It is affiliated with the New York Metropolitan Reference and Research Library Agency (METRO) and is also a participant in
the Metro Film Cooperative Program, which makes available quality films and doc-
umentaries on Latin America to the college community.

DIVISION OF INTERNATIONAL HEALTH
DEPARTMENT OF COMMUNITY MEDICINE
MOUNT SINAI SCHOOL OF MEDICINE
OF THE CITY UNIVERSITY OF NEW YORK
Annenberg Building
One Gustave L. Levy Place
New York, NY 10029
(212) 241-7941/7854

AFFILIATION
Mount Sinai Medical Center.

DEGREES AND SUBJECTS OFFERED
Four year medical training program leading to M.D. degree; post-graduate: Fellowships in International Community Medicine.

PROGRAM ACTIVITIES
Four year program includes activities that are part of the required curriculum of any medical student as well as tailor-made electives. Postgraduate program includes tailor-made curriculum to meet educational objectives of each trainee.

LIBRARY/RESEARCH FACILITIES
Mount Sinai School of Medicine Library.

NEW SCHOOL FOR SOCIAL RESEARCH
Graduate Faculty of Political
and Social Science
65 Fifth Avenue
New York, NY 10003
(212) 741-5747

21

DEGREES AND SUBJECTS OFFERED
Courses offered on Latin America deal with topics such as development policies, state formation, state and class, the Central American crisis and Latin American literature. Various levels of Spanish language courses are also offered.

LIBRARY/RESEARCH FACILITIES
Modest collection of volumes on Latin America.

NEW YORK CITY TECHNICAL COLLEGE
OF THE CITY UNIVERSITY OF NEW YORK
Puerto Rican and Latin American Studies
Namm Hall, 300 Jay Street, Room 401
Brooklyn, NY 11201
(718) 643-4595/-4689

22

AFFILIATION
The City University of New York.

DEGREES AND SUBJECTS OFFERED
Course offerings: History of Puerto Rico and Latin American History; The Puerto Rican Child in the Urban Setting and the Puerto Rican in New York City and Urban America; Latin American and Puerto Rican Literature; Puerto Rican Folklore and Social Organization of Puerto Rican Community.

LIBRARY/RESEARCH FACILITIES
New York City Technical College Library and Centro de Estudios Puertorriqueños Library.

NEW YORK UNIVERSITY
Center for Latin American
and Caribbean Studies
19 University Place, Room 310
New York, NY 10003
(212) 998-8686

AFFILIATION
Graduate School of Arts and Science, New York University.

DEGREES AND SUBJECTS OFFERED
M.A. (interdisciplinary); history, politics, literature, international business, anthropology, cinema studies, sociology.

PROGRAM ACTIVITIES
Conferences, film series, lectures.

LIBRARY/RESEARCH FACILITIES
The Elmer Holmes Bobst Library has significant holdings on Latin America and Caribbean studies as well as collections of microfilms and documents of the United Nations and other international organizations. Coverage includes the arts and humanities, social sciences and professions, and emphasizes history, politics and literature. The Center maintains a Research Program in Inter-American Affairs, with a special interest in Latin American and Caribbean migration to the New York metropolitan area.

NEW YORK UNIVERSITY
Department of Spanish and Portuguese
19 University Place, 4th Floor
New York, NY 10003
(212) 998-8770

AFFILIATION
Faculty of Arts and Sciences, Washington Square University College and Graduate School of Arts and Science.

DEGREES AND SUBJECTS OFFERED
In addition to the various Latin American (Spanish-American, Hispanic-American, Brazilian) literature majors, an undergraduate multidisciplinary nine-course Latin American Studies major is available. As many as 60 courses with a significant focus on Latin America are offered for B.A. candidates.

PROGRAM ACTIVITIES
Lectures, film festivals, conferences. The Spanish and Portuguese Department organizes events and other activities in collaboration with the Center for Latin American and Caribbean Studies.

LIBRARY/RESEARCH FACILITIES
The Elmer Bobst Library has significant holdings on Latin America and the Caribbean, as well as collections of microfilms and documents of the United Nations and other international organizations.

NEW YORK UNIVERSITY
Museum Studies Program
19 University Place, Room 308
New York, NY 10003
(212) 998-8080

AFFILIATION
New York University, Center for Latin American and Caribbean Studies.

DEGREES AND SUBJECTS OFFERED
Master of Arts in Latin American and Caribbean Studies with a concentration in Museum Studies. The program provides professional skills and internship opportunities in Museum Studies as well as substantive academic knowledge of Latin America and the Caribbean. It is aimed primarily at those who are or will be museum professionals in Latin America and the Caribbean or are specializing in collections from these areas in U.S. museums. It is open to individuals who are currently employed by museums and cultural organizations as well as to those who are newly entering the field.

LIBRARY/RESEARCH FACILITIES
Elmer Holmes Bobst Library; Museum Studies Reference Center.

PACE UNIVERSITY
Institute of Brazilian-American Business
Pace Plaza
New York, NY 10038
(212) 488-1932

AFFILIATION
Pace University.

DEGREES AND SUBJECTS OFFERED
One semester courses include: Brazilian Civilization; Caribbean Civilization; and Latin American Civilization. Seminars on Brazilian economic problems and international business problems focused on Brazil; standard undergraduate B.A. & B.S. with emphasis on business; M.B.A. degrees in graduate school with emphasis on international business, concentrating on Brazil.

PROGRAM ACTIVITIES
Conferences on special Brazilian topics, including seminars with Brazilian economists; forums with Brazilian politicians and business executives; exchange programs with Brazilian professors; special scholarship program aimed at Brazilian graduate students interested in M.B.A. degrees.

LIBRARY/RESEARCH FACILITIES
The Pace University Library has an excellent collection of books on Brazilian topics.

QUEENS COLLEGE
OF THE CITY UNIVERSITY OF NEW YORK
Latin American Area Studies
Kissena Hall
Flushing, NY 11367
(718) 520-7334/7057

AFFILIATION
The City University of New York.

DEGREES AND SUBJECTS OFFERED
B.A., M.A. degrees and Advanced Certificate in Latin American Area Studies are offered. Undergraduate students majoring in Latin American Area Studies are required to take 30 credits from the area courses and the language courses. Students may also do a joint major in Latin American Area Studies in combination with

anthropology, economics, education, history, political science, or Romance languages. The Master's degree in Latin American Area Studies is an interdisciplinary degree offered with the participation of the following departments: economics, history, political science, Romance languages and sociology. The advanced certificate program is carried out in conjunction with the above departments. The Portuguese Language and Literature Program is the only one in the CUNY system that goes beyond the introductory level.

PROGRAM ACTIVITIES
Caumsett Presidential Seminar; Latin American Week (Spring); regular forums on topics ranging from U.S.-Central America Policy Options to Afro-Brazilian Experience to Contemporary Literary Critics.

LIBRARY/RESEARCH FACILITIES
The Latin American Area Studies Library, separate from the Paul Klapper Library at Queens College, serves as a research facility for students conducting research on contemporary issues.

RUTGERS, THE STATE UNIVERSITY OF NEW JERSEY
Latin American Studies Program
Van Dyck Hall
New Brunswick, NJ 08903
(201) 932-7738/8445

28

AFFILIATION
Rutgers University, Faculty of Arts and Sciences—New Brunswick.

DEGREES AND SUBJECTS OFFERED
The interdisciplinary major in Latin American studies consists of ten term-courses (30 credits), five of which must be above the 200 level; these ten courses must include Modern Latin America (which serves as the program's general introduction to Latin American civilization), and they must be distributed among history, social sciences, and Spanish-American or Brazilian literature. Students must take a minimum of 6 credits in each of these three areas, and may count a maximum of 12 credits from each area toward the major. Majors must demonstrate language proficiency in Spanish or Portuguese.

An interdisciplinary minor in Latin American studies consists of seven courses: Modern Latin America, plus six additional courses selected from a variety of departments.

PROGRAM ACTIVITIES
Seminars, lectures, participation in conferences, concerts are organized.

LIBRARY/RESEARCH FACILITIES
Rutgers University's facility in New Brunswick:

Archibald S. Alexander Library:
169 College Avenue
College Avenue Campus
New Brunswick, NJ 08903
(201) 932-7507

RUTGERS, THE STATE UNIVERSITY OF NEW JERSEY
Department of Puerto Rican and Hispanic Caribbean Studies
Tillett Hall 237
New Brunswick, NJ 08903
(201) 932-3820/3837

AFFILIATION
Rutgers University, Faculty of Arts and Sciences–New Brunswick.

DEGREES AND SUBJECTS OFFERED
A major in Puerto Rican and Hispanic Caribbean Studies consists of ten courses (including four required courses) with special emphasis on Puerto Rican history, culture (religion, education, folklore, music, literature), economy, sociology and politics (U.S. relations with Puerto Rico). In addition, courses on the Latin American woman, Puerto Rican migration and labor, and Hispanics in the U.S. are offered, addressing issues of class conflict and development, women's roles in Hispanic societies, and all aspects of socioeconomic development.

PROGRAM ACTIVITIES
Lectures, film showings, community and cultural activities are organized.

LIBRARY/RESEARCH FACILITIES
Use of Rutgers University's campus libraries.

STATE UNIVERSITY OF NEW YORK AT STONY BROOK
Department of History
Stony Brook, NY 11794
(516) 689-6000

AFFILIATION
The State University of New York.

DEGREES AND SUBJECTS OFFERED
The History Department offers M.A. & Ph.D. degrees with concentration in Latin American history; Hispanic Languages also offers graduate degrees in Latin American literature. The Department is currently formalizing an undergraduate minor in Latin American Studies. Dozens of courses on Latin America are offered at the graduate and undergraduate levels mainly by the History, Hispanic Languages and Anthropology departments. The History Department alone has 11 regularly offered undergraduate courses on Latin America.

PROGRAM ACTIVITIES
Speakers involved in Latin American studies are invited on a regular basis. In addition, an exchange program (graduate and undergraduate) is maintained with several universities in Lima, Peru.

LIBRARY/RESEARCH FACILITIES
The library has several excellent collections of primary material for research on Brazil and Mexico. The History Department has four members whose research and teaching are in the area of Latin American Studies, making it one of the largest groups of Latin Americanists in a history department in the New York area.

YORK COLLEGE OF THE CITY UNIVERSITY OF NEW YORK
Latin American and Puerto Rican Studies
94-20 Guy R. Brewer Boulevard
Jamaica, NY 11451
(718) 262-2430

AFFILIATION
The City University of New York.

DEGREES AND SUBJECTS OFFERED
Program concentration of 21 credits in either Latin American or Puerto Rican

studies; courses in anthropology, political science, history, languages and literature, sociology, Puerto Rican society and culture, Hispanic studies, Afro-
Caribbean courses and economic development courses.

PROGRAM ACTIVITIES
Yearly forums on topics of interest concerning Latin America, e.g. discussions
among faculty, students and invited speakers on U.S. foreign policy in Latin
America, U.S. role in Grenada, situation of contemporary Nicaragua, as well as individual faculty lectures on Puerto Rican society and a Cuban film series.

LIBRARY/RESEARCH FACILITIES
Good undergraduate journal collection on the social sciences and humanities in
general and Latin American studies in particular.

ASSOCIATIONS, NONPROFIT ORGANIZATIONS, RESEARCH CENTERS

The following information was requested for each entry in this section. However, final entries contain only those categories which each organization deemed applicable.

Identification:
- Name
- Address
- Telephone

Organizational status

Parental organization/affiliation

Membership

Conditions of access

Purpose of organization

Activities/Fields of research

Research facilities

Publications

AFS INTERNATIONAL/ INTERCULTURAL PROGRAMS, INC.
313 East 43rd Street
New York, NY 10017
(212) 949-4242

32

ORGANIZATIONAL STATUS
Private, nonprofit, international educational exchange organization.

MEMBERSHIP
100,000 volunteers worldwide in 75 countries, including 22 countries in Latin America and the Caribbean.

PURPOSE OF ORGANIZATION
To promote intercultural learning through worldwide exchange programs for students, professionals, workers and families. To provide participants with knowledge, skills and values enabling them to live and work more effectively in different countries.

ACTIVITIES/FIELDS OF RESEARCH
Exchange programs in Latin American/Caribbean countries involving students (mostly at secondary levels), teachers, journalists and families.

RESEARCH FACILITIES
AFS maintains a research department whose mission is to carry out research and evaluation projects potentially leading to a better understanding of AFS exchanges; to improve AFS program implementation; to develop materials and procedures for improvement of exchange learning experience; to maintain contact with scholarly, educational and professional communities; and to serve as a consultant.

PUBLICATIONS
Almost all documents created by the AFS Research Department are available to the public free of charge. The publications are listed under the following headings: orientation handbooks and other orientation materials; occasional papers in intercultural learning; research reports; *Theory into Practice* series; miscellaneous departmental publications; externally published articles and books.

**ALL NATIONS
WOMEN'S LEAGUE, INC. (ANWL)**
*101 West 23rd Street
New York, NY 10011
(212) 989-0315*

ORGANIZATIONAL STATUS
Nonprofit volunteer organization of women.

MEMBERSHIP
Local 89 members.

CONDITIONS OF ACCESS
Reference.

PURPOSE OF ORGANIZATION
To promote a mutual understanding of women's problems and the need for community integration; to improve the cultural, educational and professional status of women throughout the world. To broaden public awareness of the goals, concerns, ideas and problems of women.

ACTIVITIES/FIELDS OF RESEARCH
Cooperation with rural farmer women in the areas of health and nutrition.

RESEARCH FACILITIES
The ANWL maintains a library.

PUBLICATIONS
Occasional.

 **THE AMERICAN BAR ASSOCIATION
Central American Goal VIII Committee
and Inter-American Law Committee**
*805 Third Avenue
New York, NY 10022
(212) 751-5700*

ORGANIZATIONAL STATUS
Professional association.

PARENTAL ORGANIZATION/AFFILIATION
American Bar Association.

PURPOSE OF ORGANIZATION
To further the rule of law in Central America. To provide information to practitioners in Latin American law.

PUBLICATIONS
The International Lawyer (quarterly); *Bulletin of the Section of International Law and Practice.*

AMERICAN FRIENDS SERVICE COMMITTEE (AFSC)
World Hunger/Global Development Program
15 Rutherford Place
New York, NY 10003
(212) 598-0963

35

ORGANIZATIONAL STATUS
Nongovernmental organization.

PARENTAL ORGANIZATION/AFFILIATION
American Friends Service Committee.

PURPOSE OF ORGANIZATION
Public education and action in the New York area on the root causes of world hunger.

ACTIVITIES/FIELDS OF RESEARCH
Public education includes problems of U.S. intervention in Central America and other factors leading to hunger in the region. *Let Them Eat Missiles*, a 25-minute slide show, and *The Hunger and Militarism Guide* both use examples from the Latin American region. Workshops for educators also include regional issues.

PUBLICATIONS
Several reports and a slide show on world hunger and militarism.

AMERICAN JEWISH COMMITTEE
International Relations Department
Office of South American Affairs
165 East 56th Street
New York, NY 10022
(212) 751-4000

36

ORGANIZATIONAL STATUS
Institute of human relations; nonprofit organization.

PURPOSE OF ORGANIZATION
To combat bigotry, protect the civil and religious rights of Jews nationally and internationally and advance the cause of improved human relations for all people everywhere.

FIELDS OF RESEARCH
Human rights, racism, anti-Semitism, Jewish communities in general, Isræli-Latin American relations and intergroup relations.

PUBLICATIONS
Commentary (monthly); *Present Tense* (quarterly); occasionally, backgrounders and research papers.

AMERICAN JEWISH CONGRESS
Commission on International Affairs
15 East 84th Street
New York, NY 10028
(212) 879-4500

ORGANIZATIONAL STATUS
Nonprofit organization.

PARENTAL ORGANIZATION/AFFILIATION
American Jewish Congress.

CONDITIONS OF ACCESS
Call in advance.

PURPOSE OF ORGANIZATION
To defend Jewish communities around the world against discrimination and abuse. To support Israel's struggle to build a land whose people can live in peace, in dignity and in security. To improve human rights and interreligious relations everywhere.

ACTIVITIES/FIELDS OF RESEARCH
Anti-Semitism; human rights; interreligious relations.

RESEARCH FACILITIES
Archives.

PUBLICATIONS
Commission on International Affairs Perspective, (irregular).

THE AMERICAS SOCIETY
680 Park Avenue
New York, NY 10021
(212) 249-8950

ORGANIZATIONAL STATUS
The Americas Society is a nonprofit, tax-exempt membership organization with an art gallery, cultural magazine and extensive educational and public affairs programs covering Latin America, the Caribbean and Canada.

MEMBERSHIP
Individual and corporate.

PARENTAL ORGANIZATION/AFFILIATION
Affiliates include the Council of the Americas, the Pan American Society of the United States, Inc., and Caribbean/Central American Action.

CONDITIONS OF ACCESS
Interest in arts and public affairs.

PURPOSE OF ORGANIZATION
The Americas Society is a national organization established to coordinate activities of other institutions concerned with hemisphere affairs in the United States. Through a broad spectrum of programs and services, the Society promotes improved understanding of the economic, political and cultural values of countries in the hemisphere and increased public awareness of the positive role of private institutions in hemisphere development.

ACTIVITIES/FIELDS OF RESEARCH
Research and activities are carried out on all countries of the hemisphere.

RESEARCH FACILITIES
Small collection of major literary works of the hemisphere, plus selection of works on Latin American studies. Working collection of periodicals on business and economy in Latin America.

PUBLICATIONS
Annual Report (once a year); *Washington Report* (bimonthly); *Update* (bimonthly newsletter); *Review Magazine* (literature and the arts; twice a year); *Calendar* (monthly listing of events).

AMERICAS WATCH COMMITTEE
36 West 44th Street
New York, NY 10036
(212) 840-9460

ORGANIZATIONAL STATUS
Nonprofit organization.

PARENTAL ORGANIZATION/AFFILIATION
Fund for Free Expression.

PURPOSE OF ORGANIZATION
To publicize violations of human rights in Central and South America and the Caribbean; to urge the U.S., other governments and international bodies to take abuses into account in devising policies and programs; to encourage members of the professions and of special interest groups to raise human rights concerns with colleagues in repressive countries.

ACTIVITIES/FIELDS OF RESEARCH
Americas Watch sponsors fact-finding missions to countries in Central and South America and the Caribbean, publishes reports on its findings, organizes public and private meetings and forums, and maintains comprehensive files on human rights violations in those countries. Americas Watch is concerned with politically motivated abuse of citizens by their governments—murder, kidnapping, emigration, censorship and deprivation of employment and political freedoms. Americas Watch carefully watches the treatment of its counterparts in other countries, especially those who have been persecuted for trying to monitor the performance of their own governments with respect to human rights. Americas Watch also evaluates the U.S. government's performance in a number of areas of human rights relevant to U.S. policy towards Latin America and the Caribbean.

RESEARCH FACILITIES
Files made available on a discretionary basis.

PUBLICATIONS
Publications on various issues such as political changes, human rights, country reports of the different Latin American and Caribbean countries are available.

AMNESTY INTERNATIONAL U.S. SECTION
322 Eighth Avenue, 10th Floor
New York, NY 10001
(212) 807-8400

40

ORGANIZATIONAL STATUS
A nongovernmental international human rights organization with over 40 country sections. The Research Department is in London; for more details on countries contact Amnesty International, 1 Easton Street, WC1X 8DJ, London, England.

MEMBERSHIP
Over 500,000 members in 150 countries, including 5,000 local groups around the world. Individuals may receive information on joining by contacting the New York office.

PURPOSE OF ORGANIZATION
Amnesty International is an international human rights organization whose membership is volunteer and which works for the release of prisoners of conscience (men and women imprisoned anywhere for their beliefs, color, religion, ethnic identity or language), and for fair and prompt trials for political prisoners as well as for an end to torture and executions.

ACTIVITIES/FIELDS OF RESEARCH
The AI Research Department in London collects documentation on human rights violations within the AI mandate for action and releases reports, papers and publications, as well as Urgent Actions on these violations. The U.S. section has copies of most publications and papers. Well over 30 Latin American and Caribbean countries are being researched in the London office. AI also has NGO status at the United Nations where the organization has presented statements to the various relevant committees on such abuses as "disappearances," extrajudicial and judicial executions, torture and the like, covering quite a number of Latin American countries.

RESEARCH FACILITIES
Papers on file may be consulted at the office. Documents may be photocopied at cost.

PUBLICATIONS
A publications catalog is available from the New York office and includes prices. Some papers on file at the office are not listed in the catalog.

ANTI-DEFAMATION LEAGUE OF B'NAI B'RITH (ADL)
Department of Latin American Affairs
823 United Nations Plaza
New York, NY 10017
(212) 490-2525

ORGANIZATIONAL STATUS
Nonprofit, nongovernmental human rights organization.

PARENTAL ORGANIZATION/AFFILIATION
Anti-Defamation League of B'nai B'rith.

PURPOSE OF ORGANIZATION
To stop the defamation of the Jewish people and to secure justice and fair treatment of all citizens alike. The Latin American Affairs Department works with the Jewish communities in Latin America to assist in developing improved intergroup/interfaith relations and combatting anti- Semitism and other forms of discrimination.

FIELDS OF RESEARCH
The promotion of human rights; community and interfaith relations; anti-Semitism; extremist groups and Latin American-Israeli relations.

RESEARCH FACILITIES
ADL's Research Department provides information on request.

PUBLICATIONS
Latin American Report (4-6 times a year) free of charge; various individual reports and articles concerning anti-Semitism and the Jewish communities of Latin America.

ARGENTINE-NORTH AMERICAN ASSOCIATION FOR THE ADVANCEMENT OF SCIENCE TECHNOLOGY AND CULTURE (ANACITEC)
210 Fifth Avenue, Suite 1102
New York, NY 10010
(212) 241-7941

ORGANIZATIONAL STATUS
Nonprofit organization.

PURPOSE OF ORGANIZATION
To promote scientific, technological and cultural cooperation between institutions and/or individuals of Argentina and the U.S.

ACTIVITIES/FIELDS OF RESEARCH
Exchanges in education and research between Argentina and the U.S.

THE ASSOCIATION OF THE BAR OF THE CITY OF NEW YORK
Committee on Inter-American Affairs
42 West 44th Street
New York, NY 10036
(212) 382-6600

ORGANIZATIONAL STATUS
Professional association.

MEMBERSHIP
U.S. and foreign members of the legal profession.

PURPOSE OF ORGANIZATION
The Association's aim is to promote reform in the law, facilitating and improving the administration of justice and elevating the standard of integrity of the legal profession. The Committee of Inter-American Affairs seeks to promote relations in the Western Hemisphere with other legal and community organizations and to address and comment on relevant issues.

ACTIVITIES/FIELDS OF RESEARCH
Reports, seminars and lectures. The Committee sometimes works in conjunction with other committees and organizations on specific subjects.

RESEARCH FACILITIES
The library of the Association is a private one, which provides services at a cost for nonmembers. It has a substantial collection of legal materials, including a collection of *International Session Laws, Codes, Case Reporters, Comparative Materials, Restatements of Foreign Laws,* the *UN Treaty Series,* selected UN documents and all materials that the Association itself has produced.

PUBLICATIONS
The Association publishes *The Record,* eight times per year. *The Record* covers some lecture series and committee reports. All lectures and reports are available through the Executive Secretary's Office.

CAMPAIGN FOR PEACE AND DEMOCRACY/ EAST AND WEST (CPD/EW)
P. O. Box 1640, Cathedral Station
New York, NY 10025
(212) 724-1157

ORGANIZATIONAL STATUS
Nonprofit political organization.

PURPOSE OF ORGANIZATION
CPD/EW brings together members of the peace movement, trade unionists, environmentalists, feminists and minority rights activists around the perspective of independence from both superpowers. CPD/EW opposes militarism, interventionism and the violation of human rights, whether in the East, West or Third World. CPD/EW is committed to building an alternative to the cold war bloc system based on movements for peace, democracy and social justice throughout the world.

ACTIVITIES/FIELDS OF RESEARCH
Issues of human rights, interventionism and social change in all Latin American countries are included in CPD/EW's main research activities.

PUBLICATIONS
Peace and Democracy News is published twice a year.

CARE
660 First Avenue
New York, NY 10016
(212) 686-3110

ORGANIZATIONAL STATUS
Voluntary, nonprofit, nongovernmental nonsectarian organization.

MEMBERSHIP
Numerous charitable and relief organizations are members of CARE.

CONDITIONS OF ACCESS
Call in advance.

PURPOSE OF ORGANIZATION
To help the developing world's poor in their efforts to achieve social and economic well-being. CARE supports processes that create competence and become self-sustaining over time. It is CARE's task to establish new standards of excellence in offering technical assistance, training, food and other material resources as well as management in combinations appropriate to local needs and priorities. CARE also advocates public policies and programs that support these ends.

ACTIVITIES/FIELDS OF RESEARCH
CARE addresses widespread malnutrition through Mother-Child Health (MCH) programs, food aid for development, health and nutrition, food production, natural resource conservation programs as well as emergency aid. In addition, CARE has identified small-enterprise development establishing new sources of employment as a means for the poor to generate income which they can use to improve their lives. CARE operates in the following Latin American countries: Belize, Bolivia, Costa Rica, the Dominican Republic, Ecuador, Guatemala, Haiti, Honduras, Mexico, Nicaragua, Panama and Peru.

PUBLICATIONS
CARE publishes several pamphlets such as *The Fact Sheet, The What and Where of CARE,* as well as an annual report in which CARE depicts its purpose, its program of activities and its audited financial statements (*Treasurer's Report*).

CARNEGIE CORPORATION OF NEW YORK
437 Madison Avenue
New York, NY 10022
(212) 371-3200

ORGANIZATIONAL STATUS
Endowed, grant-making foundation.

PURPOSE OF ORGANIZATION
The Corporation awards grants for the advancement and diffusion of knowledge and understanding among the people of the United States and of certain countries that are or have been members of the British Overseas Commonwealth.

FIELDS OF RESEARCH
A few grants are made for activities in the English-speaking Caribbean. Over the years, several grants have been made for Latin American studies in the United States, but the foundation itself does not conduct such studies.

RESEARCH FACILITIES
Grant files are available to qualified scholars doing work on specific Corporation grants.

PUBLICATIONS
Annual and quarterly reports (on grants in all fields).

CARNEGIE COUNCIL ON ETHICS AND INTERNATIONAL AFFAIRS
formerly:
Council on Religion and International Affairs
170 East 64th Street
New York, NY 10021
(212) 838-4120

ORGANIZATIONAL STATUS
Nongovernmental, public charity, educational organization.

PURPOSE OF ORGANIZATION
Founded by Andrew Carnegie in 1914, Carnegie Council has since its beginning asserted its strong belief that ethics, as informed by the world's principal religions, is an inevitable and integral component of any policy decision, whether in the realm of economics, politics or national security. The interrelationship of ethics and foreign policy is thus a unifying theme of all of Carnegie Council's programs. The Council seeks to focus on the decision-making process—the ends, means and consequences that must come into play. It tries to demystify the idea of ethics and explain it as a companion of our daily lives. By promoting greater understanding of the values and conditions that ensure peaceful relations among the nations, Carnegie Council hopes to contribute to a better life for people everywhere.

ACTIVITIES/FIELDS OF RESEARCH
The Carnegie Leadership Program, Conversations, Studies in Ethics and Foreign Policy and the *Newsletter on Church and State Abroad* address the question of Latin America to varying degrees and in many different ways. Carnegie Council's basic way of addressing questions is by providing a forum for different sides for discussion, debate and consequently, individual decision-making by the participants in its programs. Carnegie Council takes no sides on issues and does not advocate positions.

RESEARCH FACILITIES
The archives of Carnegie Council (originally called The Church Peace Union, then from 1961 to 1986 Council on Religion and International Affairs [CRIA]) are available for study at Columbia University's Library of Rare Books and Manuscripts.

PUBLICATIONS
In-house newsletter, *Ethics and International Affairs Newsletter,* and *Newsletter on Church and State Abroad* (each published approximately quarterly). Books, pamphlets and monographs intermittently.

CATHOLIC RELIEF SERVICES (CRS)
1011 First Avenue
New York, NY 10022
(212) 838-4700

48

ORGANIZATIONAL STATUS
Private nonprofit voluntary organization.

PARENTAL ORGANIZATION/AFFILIATION
United States Catholic Conference (USCC).

PURPOSE OF ORGANIZATION
To provide assistance to the poor of all countries to alleviate their immediate needs. To support self-determined community activities of people struggling to eradicate the root causes of their poverty. To help the poor preserve dignity by reaching their potential as productive human beings. To collaborate with other groups of good will in programs contributing to a just society in which all may freely participate. To help educate the people of the United States to the moral obligation to alleviate human suffering, to address its causes and to promote social justice.

FIELDS OF RESEARCH
Food aid/distribution and production programs, development (water and agriculture) program and projects. Related infrastructure activities. Most of CRS's support is to organizations and groups that might be involved in research. CRS itself is not involved in research activities.

PUBLICATIONS
Only fund-raising materials are published.

CENTER FOR COMMUNICATION, INC.
1133 Avenue of the Americas, 11th Floor
New York, NY 10036
(212) 930-4878

ORGANIZATIONAL STATUS
Nonprofit link between the academic community and communications industries.

PURPOSE OF ORGANIZATION
To create a forum of professors and students to discuss public policy issues of the communications industries with professionals working in the field.

ACTIVITIES/FIELDS OF RESEARCH
Series focusing on The Media and Human Rights in Latin America.

RESEARCH FACILITIES
Seminar transcripts; videotapes.

PUBLICATIONS
Seminar transcripts are available to the public.

CENTER FOR CUBAN STUDIES
124 West 23rd Street
New York, NY 10011
(212) 242-0559

ORGANIZATIONAL STATUS
Research center and information office.

MEMBERSHIP
Individuals, students, institutions.

CONDITIONS OF ACCESS
Open to the public.

PURPOSE OF ORGANIZATION
To disseminate accurate and up-to-date information about Cuba, given the de facto embargo on information caused by the U.S. ban on trade and travel restrictions.

ACTIVITIES/FIELDS OF RESEARCH
The Center distributes a great deal of information through its publications, film

showings, forums and exhibitions and by bringing to the U.S. a number of Cuban experts. The Center has also organized dozens of special-interest and professional visits to Cuba, and held several national conferences and symposia on Cuba. The Center has sponsored symposia on U.S.-Cuba relations in the U.S. House of Representatives and Senate.

RESEARCH FACILITIES
The library maintains a collection of approximately 4,000 books (fiction and nonfiction) and 30 serial publications that cover Cuba's culture, society, economy and history, with emphasis on the years since 1959; ten file drawers of newspaper and magazine clippings on all aspects of Cuban post-1959 society with the largest files being on health care, education, women, economy and cultural achievements. The collection includes also photograph archives, film posters and other types of Cuban art work. All material is for reference use only. Library hours: 12:00 p.m. to 5:30 p.m., Monday through Thursday.

PUBLICATIONS
The *Center for Cuban Studies Newsletter* is published ten times a year and *Cuba Update* appears bimonthly. There are occasional special publications on Cuban foreign relations, history and bilingual editions.

THE CENTER FOR DEMOCRATIC ALTERNATIVES 51
853 Broadway, Room 304
New York, NY 10003
(212) 473-3920

ORGANIZATIONAL STATUS
Nonprofit organization.

PARENTAL ORGANIZATION/AFFILIATION
Affiliated with Labor Institute.

PURPOSE OF ORGANIZATION
Newsletter survey project to involve progressive individuals/activists around the country for discussion and choice on critical issues for a common progressive agenda for the 1980s and 1990s.

FIELDS OF RESEARCH
Discussion and research on possible U.S. policies (defense, trade, etc.).

PUBLICATIONS
Newsletter (every other month). *The Progressive Agenda.*

CENTER FOR HEMISPHERIC STUDIES OF FREEDOM HOUSE
48 East 21st Street, Suite 500
New York, NY 10010
(212) 473-9691

ORGANIZATIONAL STATUS
Nongovernmental research center and information office.

CONDITIONS OF ACCESS
Information is provided through publications, and to working journalists and specialists.

PURPOSE OF ORGANIZATION
To promote and strengthen democratic institutions and the complex process of democratization in the Caribbean and Latin America.

ACTIVITIES/FIELDS OF RESEARCH
Democratization, human rights and strategic issues.

PUBLICATIONS
Articles on the Caribbean and Latin America appear regularly in *Freedom at Issue,* the Freedom House journal which appears six times a year. The Center's analyses also appear in Freedom House's monograph series which includes *El Salvador: Peaceful Revolution or Armed Struggle* by R. Bruce McColm, as well as *The Democratic Mask: The Consolidation of the Sandinista Revolution* by Douglas W. Payne. Occasional special reports on the region are also issued.

THE CINEMA GUILD
1697 Broadway, Room 802
New York, NY 10019
(212) 246-5522

ORGANIZATIONAL STATUS
Film and video distributor.

PARENTAL ORGANIZATION/AFFILIATION
The Cinema Guild Inc.

PURPOSE OF ORGANIZATION
To provide films and videotapes on Latin American and Caribbean topics for academic and other non-theatrical film/video users.

PUBLICATIONS
Various catalogs and brochures available on request, currently including The Cinema Guild Film and Video Catalog (describing over 300 titles in a wide range of academic disciplines), The Cinema Guild Feature Film Catalog (describing several dozen narrative and documentary feature-length films), and a Cuban Film Archive brochure.

COALITION OF CITIZENS FOR CUBAN-AMERICANS, INC.
New School for Social Research
Human Resources Department
65 Fifth Avenue
New York, NY 10003
(212) 741-7757

ORGANIZATIONAL STATUS
Community services and advocacy-oriented organization.

PURPOSE OF ORGANIZATION
To assist newly arrived Cuban refugees in adapting to life in the U.S.

ACTIVITIES/FIELDS OF RESEARCH
Periodic preparation of position papers for the orientation of public and nonprofit service agencies dealing with issues confronting newly arrived Cuban refugees in the Greater New York area.

COMMITTEE IN SOLIDARITY WITH THE PEOPLE OF GUATEMALA (CSPG)
225 Lafayette Street, Room 212
New York, NY 10012
(212) 219-2704

ORGANIZATIONAL STATUS
Solidarity organization; information office.

PURPOSE OF ORGANIZATION
To provide information about the current political, economic, social and human

rights situation in Guatemala, as well as an historical perspective; to organize support for the struggles of the people of Guatemala for economic and social justice and self-determination.

ACTIVITIES/FIELDS OF RESEARCH
Historical and current political, economic, social and human rights issues as well as social justice and self-determination in Guatemala; United States foreign policy in Guatemala and the Central American region.

RESEARCH FACILITIES
The Committee has collections of various periodicals and publications on Guatemala.

PUBLICATIONS
Update on Guatemala, published monthly (news events in Guatemala; articles on U.S. policy regarding Guatemala).

 COMMITTEE TO PROTECT JOURNALISTS (CPJ)
36 West 44th Street, Room 911
New York, NY 10036
(212) 944-7216

ORGANIZATIONAL STATUS
Nonprofit, nonpartisan membership organization and information clearinghouse.

MEMBERSHIP
Open to journalists and other persons engaged in the business of gathering and reporting the news.

PURPOSE OF ORGANIZATION
To support the human and professional rights of journalists around the world.

PUBLICATIONS
The CPJ Update Newsletter is published on a bimonthly basis. A list of additional publications is available upon request.

COUNCIL OF THE AMERICAS
680 Park Avenue
New York, NY 10021
(212) 249-8950

57

ORGANIZATIONAL STATUS
Business advocacy organization.

PARENTAL ORGANIZATION/AFFILIATION
The Americas Society.

MEMBERSHIP
Corporate.

CONDITIONS OF ACCESS
U.S. corporations dealing with Latin America.

PURPOSE OF ORGANIZATION
The Council of the Americas is a U.S. business association of companies with interests in Latin America and the Caribbean. The Council's activities bring its corporate member executives together with Latin American and U.S. government officials to improve the understanding and foster acceptance of the role that U.S. private enterprise plays in the region's economic development. The Council also facilitates private sector-to-private sector interchange through country- and issue-specific business roundtables and its sponsorship of the U.S. Council of the Mexico-U.S. Business Committee, a binational organization linking the U.S. and Mexican private sectors.

ACTIVITIES/FIELDS OF RESEARCH
Research is carried out on all countries of the hemisphere.

RESEARCH FACILITIES
Small collection of major literary works of the hemisphere, plus selection of works on Latin American studies. Working collection of periodicals on business and economy in Latin America.

PUBLICATIONS
Annual Report (once a year); *Washington Report* (bimonthly); *Update* (bimonthly newsletter); *Review Magazine* (literature and the arts; twice a year); *Calendar* (monthly listing of events).

COUNCIL ON FOREIGN RELATIONS
58 East 68th Street
New York, NY 10021
(212) 734-0400

ORGANIZATIONAL STATUS
Nongovernmental organization.

MEMBERSHIP
Membership association; nomination and seconding by members.

PURPOSE OF ORGANIZATION
To break new ground in the consideration of international issues; to help shape American foreign policy in a constructive, non- partisan manner and to inform and stimulate the Council's membership as well as to reach a wider audience through publications and other means.

ACTIVITIES/FIELDS OF RESEARCH
In Latin American Program: Latin American immigration and U.S. foreign policy; U.S.-Cuba relations; U.S. relations with Central America; U.S. relations with the advanced developing countries of Latin America; U.S.-Mexico relations.

RESEARCH FACILITIES
Library (reference collection). Open to members only, or their guests.

PUBLICATIONS
The main publication of the Council is *Foreign Affairs Magazine.* The Council also has an extensive publication program. The Latin American Program has to date one major publication: *Latin Migration North* by Michæl Teitelbaum. Subsequent publications on U.S.-Cuban policy, U.S. relations with the advanced developing countries, Congress and Central American policy and the new Latin American democracies and their future prospects, will be published within the next year or two.

COUNCIL ON INTERNATIONAL AND PUBLIC AFFAIRS
777 United Nations Plaza
New York, NY 10017
(212) 972-9877

ORGANIZATIONAL STATUS
Nongovernmental organization.

PURPOSE OF ORGANIZATION
Through its program on Technology and Work the Council is examining the impact of frontier technologies (especially biotechnology) on developing countries.

ACTIVITIES/FIELDS OF RESEARCH
With the International Center for Law in Development, the Council has organized workshops in Brazil and Mexico on biotechnology and its impact on Third World societies.

RESEARCH FACILITIES
The Council has material on biotechnology and on impacts of hazardous industries (especially relating to the Bhopal disaster in India).

PUBLICATIONS
The Council operates several publishing programs and has papers available describing activities on biotechnology, including reports of the workshops held in Brazil and Mexico.

CUBAN NATIONAL PLANNING COUNCIL (CNPC)
New York Office
34-48 70th Street
Jackson Heights, NY 11372
(718) 898-3601

ORGANIZATIONAL STATUS
National Office: community service, research; New York Office: information and referral.

PARENTAL ORGANIZATION/AFFILIATION
Cuban National Planning Council, Inc.

CONDITIONS OF ACCESS
By resolution of the Board of Directors.

PURPOSE OF ORGANIZATION
To promote the socioeconomic well-being of Cuban Americans and others in need.

FIELDS OF RESEARCH
Policy research and analysis on socioeconomic issues related to the Cuban-American community; Hispanic Leadership Training Program to increase participation by Hispanics in boards and committees in the public and private sectors; Resettlement Program designed to service Cuban refugees; and Hands Across the Campus, a program operated in collaboration with the American Jewish Committee in Dade County, Florida.

RESEARCH FACILITIES
The New York Office of the CNPC has a reference collection on Cuban Americans. Orientation and referral information for research on Cuban Americans.

PUBLICATIONS
CNPC Newsletter is published quarterly from Miami by the Cuban-American Policy Center, a program of the CNPC. Copies are available at the New York office of CNPC. *CNPC Issue Paper,* occasional publication on selected issues.

 DOMINICAN INSTITUTE
FOR RESEARCH AND SOCIAL ACTION, INC.
506 West 177th Street
New York, NY 10033
(212) 927-8904

ORGANIZATIONAL STATUS
Nonprofit organization.

PURPOSE OF ORGANIZATION
Social research on the Dominican community in the U. S. as a basis to develop policies (educational, training, employment, health, and culture).

FORD FOUNDATION
320 East 43rd Street
New York, NY 10017
(212) 573-5000

ORGANIZATIONAL STATUS
Foundation.

PURPOSE OF ORGANIZATION
Grant-making institution.

ACTIVITIES/FIELDS OF RESEARCH
In Latin America and the Caribbean, the Foundation provides funding primarily to institutions based in the region in the areas of Rural Poverty and Resources, Urban Poverty, Human Rights and Social Justice, Governance and Public Policy, International Affairs, Education and Culture.

RESEARCH FACILITIES
No specialized Latin American collection. Library access for those outside the Foundation by referral only.

PUBLICATIONS
Occasional program reports.

FOREIGN POLICY ASSOCIATION (FPA)
729 Seventh Avenue
New York, NY 10019
(212) 764-4050

ORGANIZATIONAL STATUS
Nonprofit, nonpartisan educational organization.

PURPOSE OF ORGANIZATION
Citizen education in world affairs.

ACTIVITIES/FIELDS OF RESEARCH
Distinguished representatives from Latin America and the Caribbean area and U.S. government officials concerned with foreign policy toward the region frequently address FPA audiences.

RESEARCH FACILITIES
The FPA has a small library for staff use only.

PUBLICATIONS
The 1986 publication, *Great Decisions*, a 96- page briefing book on eight foreign policy topics, prepared by the editors of the FPA with critical review by experts, includes articles on *How Foreign Policy is Made: The Case of Central America; Democracy in Latin America: Focus on Argentina and Brazil;* and *Third World Development: Old Problems, New Strategies.* The series appears on an annual basis. The collection *Headline Series* is written by outside experts and published by FPA five times a year. Recent titles relating to Latin America and the Caribbean include: *Brazil and the U.S.; Third World Radical Regimes: Policy Under Carter and Reagan; Central America: Current Crisis and Future Prospects; Mexico: Neighbor in Transition;* and *The Puerto Rican Question.* Special issues such as *Mexico: The Quest for a U.S. Policy,* are done occasionally.

THE FOUNDATION CENTER
79 Fifth Avenue
New York, NY 10003
(212) 620-4230

ORGANIZATIONAL STATUS
Independent, nonprofit organization.

PURPOSE OF ORGANIZATION
The Center is a national service organization established by foundations to provide an authoritative source of information on private philanthropic giving. The Center disseminates information on private giving through public service programs, publications and through a national network of library reference collections for free public use.

ACTIVITIES/FIELDS OF RESEARCH
The Center provides an extensive public service and education program through its four libraries and its national network of over 170 cooperating collections.

RESEARCH FACILITIES
The Center has two national libraries (one at this address in New York and the other at 1001 Connecticut Avenue, N.W., Washington D.C. 20036) and two field offices (San Francisco, CA and Cleveland, OH). The libraries provide access to all of the Center's publications, plus a wide range of other books, services, periodicals, and research documents relating to foundations and philanthropy. The Center also supplies its publications and supplemental resources to cooperating collections in over 170 libraries throughout the U. S., Canada, Mexico, Puerto Rico, the Virgin Islands and Great Britain.

PUBLICATIONS
All corporate, community, and private foundations actively engaged in grantmaking, regardless of size or geographic location, are included in one or more of the Center's publications. Many fund research and programs on Latin America. There are directories that describe specific grantmakers characterizing their program interests and providing fiscal and personnel data; grant indexes that list and classify by subject recent foundation awards; and guides and related materials which introduce the reader to funding research and proposal writing.

THE FUND FOR FREE EXPRESSION
36 West 44th Street, Suite 911
New York, NY 10036
(212) 840-9460

ORGANIZATIONAL STATUS
Nonprofit organization.

PARENTAL ORGANIZATION/AFFILIATION
The Fund is the parent organization of Americas Watch, Helsinki Watch and Asia Watch.

CONDITIONS OF ACCESS
By appointment.

PURPOSE OF ORGANIZATION
To aid in the worldwide struggle by authors, journalists and all other individuals to speak without fear of reprisal. Journalists, writers, editors, publishers and concerned citizens dedicated to preserve intellectual freedom throughout the world participate.

ACTIVITIES/FIELDS OF RESEARCH
Intervention on behalf of Latin American individuals barred from the U.S. Occasional projects on specific Latin American issues are sponsored.

RESEARCH FACILITIES
The Fund maintains its own publications.

PUBLICATIONS
With other Watch committees, the Fund publishes 20 to 30 reports yearly. Bimonthly *Newsletter*.

THE FUND FOR PEACE
345 East 46th Street, Room 207
New York, NY 10017
(212) 661-5900

ORGANIZATIONAL STATUS
Independent nonprofit organization.

CONDITIONS OF ACCESS
By appointment.

PURPOSE OF ORGANIZATION
To promote greater knowledge and understanding of global problems that threaten human survival. The organization is dedicated to the elimination of war as a means of settling international disputes, and to the attainment of a just, free, and peaceful world.

ACTIVITIES/FIELDS OF RESEARCH
The Fund for Peace works through a national office located in New York which provides back-up funding, administrative support, and coordination for the Fund's operational units and undertakes special projects relating to peace and international security. The Fund's four major projects are located in Washington D.C.: the Center for International Policy analyzes the impact of U.S. foreign policies on human rights and social and economic conditions in the Third World; the Center for National Security Studies monitors the practices of U.S. intelligence agencies and alerts Congress and the public to violations of civil liberties in the name of national security and to efforts at covert intervention; the Center for Defense Information is a nonpartisan research organization that provides objective analyses of U.S. military programs for members of Congress, top decision makers, the news media, key opinion leaders and individuals and groups throughout the U.S.; *In the Public Interest* is a daily program of radio commentaries on national and international affairs which serves as the voice of the Fund for Peace. The Institute for the Study of World Politics, located in New York, awards fellowships in an annual competition to assist scholars to obtain advanced degrees and become effective analysts, teachers, and writers on problems of peace and international security.

PUBLICATIONS
The Jœl Brooke Memorial Committee, established in 1982 to honor the fund's late President, publishes an annotated directory of resources on the subject of peace.

For additional publication lists contact the national office.

HISPANIC POLICY DEVELOPMENT PROJECT (HPDP)
250 Park Avenue South, Suite 5000A
New York, NY 10003
(212) 529-9323

ORGANIZATIONAL STATUS
Publicly supported organization.

PURPOSE OF ORGANIZATION
To provide accurate information about U.S. Hispanics and to encourage the analysis of public policies and policy proposals affecting Hispanics.

PUBLICATIONS
Publications are available from HPDP, with multiple copy discounts. These include fact books and reports on social, economic and political data on Hispanics in the U.S. For information on publications, contact:

Hispanic Policy Development Project
1001 Connecticut Avenue, N.W., Suite 310
Washington, D.C. 20036
(202) 822-8414.

THE HISPANIC SOCIETY OF AMERICA
613 West 155th Street
New York, NY 10032
(212) 926-2234

ORGANIZATIONAL STATUS
Research institution, museum, and library, founded in 1904.

MEMBERSHIP
Honorary.

CONDITIONS OF ACCESS
Museum open to the general public; library open to qualified scholars.

PURPOSE OF ORGANIZATION
To establish a free public museum and reference library to present the culture of Hispanic peoples.

FIELDS OF RESEARCH
Edward L. Tinker Pre-Doctoral Fellowship for Spanish Colonial Studies. Continuing exhibitions and publications on Spanish colonial subjects.

RESEARCH FACILITIES
Extensive manuscript collection on Colonial Spanish America as well as early books and related modern books.

PUBLICATIONS
Numerous doctoral dissertations completed at American and Latin American universities pursuant to the aforementioned fellowship. A publications list is available upon request.

 INSTITUTE OF INTERNATIONAL EDUCATION (IIE)
809 United Nations Plaza
New York, NY 10017
(212) 984-5413

ORGANIZATIONAL STATUS
Information office. IIE is the largest and most active higher educational exchange agency in the United States.

CONDITIONS OF ACCESS
Open to students interested in studies in Latin America, U.S. educators interested in teaching abroad, diplomatic personnel, employees of multinational corporations and their families and others.

PURPOSE OF ORGANIZATION
To provide information about international educational exchange to students, educators and adult learners in the New York metropolitan area.

RESEARCH FACILITIES
The Institute's resources include catalogs from universities in Latin America and the Caribbean area as well as information on study programs relating to these areas. In addition the Institute has its own family of guidebooks to higher educational exchange for purchase and consultation. These include the Learning Traveler guide to study-abroad programs for U.S. nationals, and a series of guides for foreign nationals, which includes Specialized Study Options U.S.A. and English Language and Orientation Programs in the United States. The IIE administers the

Fulbright Program of USIA at predoctoral level for both U.S. and foreign graduate students in Latin America and the Caribbean, and fellowship programs for USAID, Government of Brazil, World Bank and other sponsors which also involve training of Latin American and Caribbean nationals.

PUBLICATIONS
Informational brochures, IIE guidebooks, U.S. and foreign university catalogs, materials on scholarships and grants for international exchange, career opportunities in international education, internships and volunteer programs, teaching abroad and in the U.S. and others.

INSTITUTE OF PUBLIC ADMINISTRATION (IPA)
55 West 44th Street
New York, NY 10036
(212) 730-5480

ORGANIZATIONAL STATUS
Nonprofit research, education and consulting organization.

PURPOSE OF ORGANIZATION
To promote strengthened management and organization of governments through a program of research, education and consulting.

ACTIVITIES/FIELDS OF RESEARCH
Broad range of basic and applied research and consulting on selected topics including government structure, management and inter-governmental relations, fiscal management, taxation, transportation, management development, personnel and training. IPA's clients include state and local governments in the U.S., the federal government, foreign governments (Asia, Africa, Latin America) and international aid agencies. Work is funded by endowment and contracts.

RESEARCH FACILITIES
The library contains over 50,000 volumes. It is the oldest public administration library in the U.S. The library is used primarily for IPA staff research and may be used by scholars on request to the Librarian.

PUBLICATIONS
IPA Report; brochures on IPA services; annotated bibliographies; selected IPA Library acquisitions; studies and reports.

71 INTERNATIONAL LEAGUE FOR HUMAN RIGHTS
432 Park Avenue South
New York, NY 10016
(212) 629-6170

ORGANIZATIONAL STATUS
Nongovernmental organization.

PURPOSE OF ORGANIZATION
To promote and to protect internationally guaranteed human rights as enumerated in the Universal Declaration of Human Rights and the International Covenants. To protect human rights defenders worldwide who become the victims of repression because of their efforts to aid others.

ACTIVITIES/FIELDS OF RESEARCH
Occasional fact-finding missions; issue of reports; aid to domestically based affiliates. The league has affiliates in the following countries in Latin America: Argentina, Chile, Jamaica, Nicaragua, Paraguay and Uruguay.

RESEARCH FACILITIES
The League's library includes international human rights documentation, including United Nations materials (among which, reports of Latin American countries to the United Nations Human Rights Committee) and some OAS documents. Also many holdings from Latin American human rights organizations.

PUBLICATIONS
Human Rights Bulletin (quarterly); mission (or other) reports: *Paraguay* (4) including Mbareté (1979, available in English and Spanish); *Chile: News from the Chilean Commission for Human Rights* (8 issues to date, occasional, in English); *Uruguay's Human Rights Record* (1982) and *Nicaragua's Indians* (1983).

72 LATIN AMERICAN-CARIBBEAN LABOR INSTITUTE, INC. (LALI)
34-48 70th Street
Jackson Heights, NY 11372
(718) 898-3601

ORGANIZATIONAL STATUS
Nonprofit institute.

CONDITIONS OF ACCESS
By decision of the Board of Directors.

PURPOSE OF ORGANIZATION
To promote research, exchange of visits, publications, conferences, technical and financial assistance and all activities that will benefit labor in Latin America and the Caribbean.

ACTIVITIES/FIELDS OF RESEARCH
Latin American labor, including rural and urban workers, peasants associations, Indian communities. Relations between the U. S. and Latin American-Caribbean labor movements. Economic, social, political and cultural issues and trends that relate to Latin American-Caribbean labor. Fundraising activities to support democratic labor organizations in Latin America.

RESEARCH FACILITIES
Latin American-Caribbean labor periodicals and books.

PUBLICATIONS
Quarterly bulletin.

LAWYERS COMMITTEE FOR HUMAN RIGHTS
330 Seventh Avenue, 10th Floor North
New York, NY 10001
(212) 629-6170

73

ORGANIZATIONAL STATUS
Nonprofit, nonpartisan human rights organization and Public Interest Law Center.

CONDITIONS OF ACCESS
Write or telephone in advance.

PURPOSE OF ORGANIZATION
As an organization with an international focus, the Lawyers Committee reports on violations of human rights wherever they occur. The committee's reports are almost always based on the findings of investigative missions to the country. As an organization based in the United States, the Committee closely monitors the U.S. government's human rights policies towards countries that receive foreign aid. The committee evaluates all countries against a single standard embodied in the Universal Declaration of Human Rights. Domestic efforts center on U.S. refugee policy. The committee arranges pro bono legal representation for indigent asylum seekers and has taken on a number of class action law suits.

FIELDS OF RESEARCH
Human rights reporting; representation of asylum applicants, and testimony before the United States Congress on human rights violations in the region.

RESEARCH FACILITIES
The Lawyers Committee retains country files on every country in Latin America. The files include news clippings and reports issued by other organizations. The Committee has prepared videotapes designed for lawyers representing asylum applicants on the conditions in Haiti, El Salvador and Guatemala. These videotapes are available to the general public.

PUBLICATIONS
A newsletter is published on a quarterly basis. Recent publications include reports on El Salvador, Haiti, Honduras, Nicaragua and Uruguay. Other publications include reports on Argentina; U.S. Human Rights Policy; Reports to the United Nations on Peru and Nicaragua; Immigration, Refugees and Asylum Reports including Immigration Reform Legislation, Reports on Refugees and Asylum, and Training Materials. All publications are available for purchase by contacting the Committee.

MEDIA NETWORK
The Alternative Media Information Center
121 Fulton Street, 5th Floor
New York, NY 10038
(212) 619-3455

ORGANIZATIONAL STATUS
Nonprofit information clearinghouse on social-issue films and videos.

MEMBERSHIP
600.

CONDITIONS OF ACCESS
Phone requests for information on film; nominal charge for extensive searches (all services free to members).

PURPOSE OF ORGANIZATION
To increase public awareness of how media define and influence our lives; to help people who are working for social change identify and use films, videotapes and slideshows to further their goals; to introduce quality independently produced media to a broader audience.

ACTIVITIES/FIELDS OF RESEARCH
The Center maintains a computerized information clearinghouse on films on a wide variety of issues including Latin America.

RESEARCH FACILITIES
Most comprehensive information source on independent film and media on social issues. A computerized data base on social issues film is available for purchase and can be accessed over the phone.

PUBLICATIONS
Quarterly newsletter and other publications, among them *Guide to Films on Central America.*

MUSEUM OF THE AMERICAN INDIAN HEYE FOUNDATION 75
Broadway and 155th Street
New York, NY 10032
(212) 283-2420

ORGANIZATIONAL STATUS
Anthropological museum.

CONDITIONS OF ACCESS
Curatorial permission.

PURPOSE OF ORGANIZATION
The study of anthropology, in particular that relating to the aboriginal peoples of the Western Hemisphere.

ACTIVITIES/FIELDS OF RESEARCH
Collection, preservation, exhibition and study of all things connected with the anthropology of the aboriginal peoples of the Americas.

RESEARCH FACILITIES
Artifact collection of approximately one million items; photo archive of some 70,000 prints, negatives and transparencies; library of about 40,000 volumes.

PUBLICATIONS
Irregular.

**NATIONAL ACTION COUNCIL
FOR MINORITIES IN ENGINEERING, INC.
(NACME)**
*3 West 35th Street
New York, NY 10001
(212) 279-2626*

ORGANIZATIONAL STATUS
Nonprofit professional association.

PURPOSE OF ORGANIZATION
NACME was founded to act as a catalyst in the minority engineering education effort. This movement, which was started more than a decade ago by companies,
educators, professional societies and minority organizations, strives to increase
the number of under-represented minorities who graduate from accredited engineering schools.

ACTIVITIES/FIELDS OF RESEARCH
As an enabling organization, NACME serves as a national focal point to initiate, facilitate and develop both programs and services that support Blacks, Mexican
Americans, Puerto Ricans and American Indians on an educational path leading
to a baccalaureate degree in engineering. These activities include: (1) the Incen-
tive Grants program, the nation's largest privately supported source of scholarships for minority engineering students; (2) a field services program that offers
technical assistance, data and statistics collection and grants placement; and (3)
an active publications program.

RESEARCH FACILITIES
NACME maintains an active data file and issues publication enrollment, graduation and retention figures of Mexican Americans and Puerto Ricans enrolled in
engineering education. Files are available to scholars who are interested in research issues in this area.

PUBLICATIONS
*Annual Report; Quarterly Newsletter; Student Guide to Engineering Schools; Fi-
nancial Aid Handbook; Design for Excellence: How to Study Smartly; Minorities in
Engineering* (pamphlet); *Improving the Retention and Graduation of Minorities in
Engineering.*

NATIONAL COMMITTEE ON AMERICAN FOREIGN POLICY, INC.
211 East 43rd Street, Room 2302
New York, NY 10017
(212) 685-3411

77

ORGANIZATIONAL STATUS
Nongovernmental organization.

MEMBERSHIP
U.S. diplomats and leaders in education, finance, industry and communications (300).

CONDITIONS OF ACCESS
Open. Payment of membership dues.

PURPOSE OF ORGANIZATION
To stimulate interest in the serious problems confronting the United States in its foreign relations. The National Committee's principal concerns include the preservation and strengthening of open-society countries everywhere and the forging of an open-society bloc; the competition between East and West; the furthering of human rights; the problems of the Third World; nuclear proliferation and arms control; the problems of global resources.

ACTIVITIES/FIELDS OF RESEARCH
Fact finding missions to the Panama Canal and other key areas of Central America; conferences, symposia and seminars on Central America.

RESEARCH FACILITIES
The National Committee does not have its own library. It uses the resources of the CUNY Graduate School, the New York Public Library and other important collections in the New York City area. The Newsletter and books published by the organization and/or its members are available for reference in the office of the Committee.

PUBLICATIONS
Newsletter, published six times a year, includes important articles on issues of American foreign policy, including those concerned with Latin America and the Caribbean. Books published by Greenwood Press and Westview Press, including conference papers and special volumes.

THE NATIONAL CONFERENCE
OF CHRISTIANS AND JEWS, INC. (NCCJ)
71 Fifth Avenue
New York, NY 10003
(212) 206-0006

ORGANIZATIONAL STATUS
Human relations civic organization.

MEMBERSHIP
300 national trustees, 2000 regional.

PURPOSE OF ORGANIZATION
To promote individual and group self-dignity, cooperation, mutual understanding and respect among all peoples. The NCCJ strives to eliminate prejudices which disfigure and distort religious, business, social and political relations. It seeks to achieve a society in which the ideals of equity and justice shall become the standards of human relationships.

PUBLICATIONS
Annual Report; Program Notes (quarterly); *Newsletter* (biannually); *The Human Family...Understanding Other People* (annually); *A Calendar of Religious and Ethnic Festivals* (annually).

NATIONAL COUNCIL OF THE CHURCHES
OF CHRIST IN THE U.S.A. (NCCC)
Latin American and Caribbean Office
475 Riverside Drive, Room 622
New York, NY 10115-0050
(212) 870-2460/61/62

ORGANIZATIONAL STATUS
Nonprofit organization.

PURPOSE OF ORGANIZATION
As part of the National Council of the Churches of Christ, the aim of the Caribbean and Latin American Office is to strive for peace and justice in the social, political and economic order; act as responsible servants to people in need; foster education about and for ecumenism and engage in all educational efforts from an ecu-

menical perspective; nurture ecumenical life through relationships with local, regional, national and world ecumenical bodies, and groups and movements of Christians seeking renewal and unity; and cultivate relationships and dialogue with people of other faiths and ideologies. NCCC's mandate brings into focus humanitarian assistance in many forms, advocacy for improved U.S. foreign and economic policies, and Church World Service efforts with colleague agencies throughout the region. The purpose of NCCC is to carry out refugee resettlement, overseas ministries of evangelism, education, healing, disaster relief, and development aid that helps people achieve self-sufficiency. Additional projects include future planning for programs, press and broadcast dissemination of NCCC's objectives.

FIELDS OF RESEARCH
Ecumenical programs and projects with colleague organizations through regional representatives supported by NCCC's Caribbean and Latin American Office include development, nutritional, material assistance and material resource programs.

PUBLICATIONS
Annual reports; Church World Service publications; Studies (e.g. religious sects in Latin America and the Caribbean; economic situation).

NATIONAL COUNCIL ON INTERNATIONAL TRADE DOCUMENTATION
350 Broadway, Suite 205
New York, NY 10013
(212) 925-1400

ORGANIZATIONAL STATUS
Nonprofit membership organization.

MEMBERSHIP
Companies, associations, individuals.

CONDITIONS OF ACCESS
Payment of membership fees, depending on size of organization.

PURPOSE OF ORGANIZATION
To simplify and improve international trade documentation and procedures, including information exchange by either paper or electronic methods.

ACTIVITIES/FIELDS OF RESEARCH
Consular documentation, including consular invoices, visas and fees. Elimination of trade barriers relative to certificate standards; inventories of chemical substances; inspection procedures. Elimination of certificates of origin and incorporating information in the commercial invoice. Related subjects.

RESEARCH FACILITIES
Publications on international trade facilitation. Technical committees of experts, approximately 400 in number, from member companies which treat a multiplicity of international trade facilitation matters.

PUBLICATIONS
Annual journal-report.

NATIONAL FILM BOARD OF CANADA
1251 Avenue of the Americas, 16th Floor
New York, NY 10020
(212) 586-5131

ORGANIZATIONAL STATUS
Film agency of the government of Canada.

PURPOSE OF ORGANIZATION
To produce and distribute socially and culturally relevant films.

ACTIVITIES/FIELDS OF RESEARCH
Films have been produced on Latin America and the Caribbean in both French and English, including *Richesse des Autres, Dream of a Free Country, Waiting for Fidel* and many others.

RESEARCH FACILITIES
Films are made available through U.S. film distributors, direct sale and rental library.

PUBLICATIONS
Yearly catalog.

NATIONAL LAWYERS GUILD
NEW YORK CITY CHAPTER
Central America Task Force (CATF)
853 Broadway, Room 1701
New York, NY 10003
(212) 966-9494

82

ORGANIZATIONAL STATUS
Professional association.

PARENTAL ORGANIZATION/ AFFILIATION
National Lawyers Guild (NLG).

MEMBERSHIP
Lawyers, law students, legal workers.

PURPOSE OF ORGANIZATION
To educate our members and the community at large about U.S. policies of intervention in Central America and the Caribbean and to challenge the legality of those policies through judicial, legislative and educational action.

ACTIVITIES/FIELDS OF RESEARCH
Educational forums on U.S. policies in Central America and the Caribbean; delegations to Central America and published reports on findings; litigation challenging U.S. policies in Central America and the Caribbean illustrating government violations of international and domestic laws; legal representation of refugees seeking political asylum and those giving sanctuary to them.

PUBLICATIONS
Legal, political and issue-specific reports on Central American and Caribbean area countries are available.

NATIONAL PUERTO RICAN FORUM
31 East 32nd Street
New York, NY 10016
(212) 685-2311

83

ORGANIZATIONAL STATUS
Nonprofit organization. Employment and training programs for the economically disadvantaged. Professional placement and orientation.

PURPOSE OF ORGANIZATION
To eliminate employment barriers, to implement affirmative action, and in general, to advance the Puerto Rican and Hispanic community.

PUBLICATIONS
General studies on poverty conditions of Puerto Ricans in New York and the U.S. and cost effectiveness of training and employment for welfare recipients.

NEW JEWISH AGENDA
64 Fulton Street, No.1100
New York, NY 10038
(212) 227-5885

ORGANIZATIONAL STATUS
Nonprofit political educational organization.

MEMBERSHIP
Subscribers, Members, Sustainers.

PURPOSE OF ORGANIZATION
Agenda tries to be a progressive force in the Jewish community and a Jewish voice in the progressive community. Priority issues include peace and justice in the Middle East and Central America, feminism, disarmament, economic and social justice, lesbian and gay rights, and opposition to racism, anti-Semitism and apartheid.

ACTIVITIES/FIELDS OF RESEARCH
Investigation of the Reagan administration's charges of anti-Semitism against the Sandinista government; continuous work on Israel and arms sales to Central America; ongoing file of synagogues, Jewish organizations and prayer groups that have declared Sanctuary for Central American refugees.

RESEARCH FACILITIES
Press files on Nicaragua and the anti-Semitism issue and work done on the Sanctuary movement.

PUBLICATIONS
The Jewish Human Rights Delegation Report to Nicaragua, August 1984; *Jews and the Sanctuary Movement* (ongoing brochure); *Jews and Central America* (ongoing brochure); *Quarterly Newsletter.*

NEW YORK CIRCUS, INC. (NYC)
P.O. Box 37, Times Square Station
New York, NY 10108
(212) 928-7600

85

ORGANIZATIONAL STATUS
Nonprofit religious organization.

PURPOSE OF ORGANIZATION
To minister on a daily basis within the Latin American community in New York; to operate a research, documentation and action center for social justice and international awareness; to provide educational materials on the life and struggles of the contemporary church, with a focus on the Popular Church in Latin America.

FIELDS OF RESEARCH
Emphasis is put on the Popular Church in Chile, El Salvador, Honduras, Guatemala and Nicaragua.

RESEARCH FACILITIES
Approximately 450 books and 45 regular periodicals are maintained.

PUBLICATIONS
Lucha Struggle Journal. A listing of the books published by NYC is available on request.

NORTH AMERICAN CONGRESS ON LATIN AMERICA (NACLA)
475 Riverside Drive, Rm. 249
New York, NY 10115
(212) 870-3146

ORGANIZATIONAL STATUS
Nongovernmental research institute; publisher.

PURPOSE OF ORGANIZATION
To study, analyze and educate a general interest and specialist constituency about the historic relationship of the United States to the nations of the Western Hemisphere; to investigate the history, development and articulation of U.S. hemispheric policy; to study and explain alternative forms of political/economic/social development as they emerge throughout the hemisphere.

FIELDS OF RESEARCH
Current work: Political analysis of Central America with special emphasis on El Salvador, Guatemala, Nicaragua, including U.S. policy, existing governments and insurgency movements; U.S. military policy in the Caribbean; the role of evangelical protestantism and current Vatican foreign policy in Central America; the role of the Soviet Union in the Western Hemisphere.

RESEARCH FACILITIES
Research library, open to the public by appointment only: 1:30pm-5:30pm, Monday through Friday. A small fee is charged for use of the facilities. The library contains an extensive collection of U.S. Latin American and Caribbean periodicals, especially from the political left; books; newspaper clippings from major U.S. newspapers on all countries of the hemisphere from 1971 to the present; and FBIS, 1981-present.

PUBLICATIONS
NACLA Report on the Americas: Bimonthly journal, featuring in-depth study of a particular theme, using a political/economic approach, journalistic articles on particular countries, book review. Recent issues: *Latin American Debt; Sandinista International Relations; U.S. Military Policy in the Caribbean; Vatican Policy in Central America.*

NORTHEAST HISPANIC CATHOLIC CENTER
1011 First Avenue, Room 1233
New York, NY
(212) 751-7045

ORGANIZATIONAL STATUS
Interstate regional pastoral center.

PARENTAL ORGANIZATION/AFFILIATION
U.S. Conference of Catholic Bishops.

CONDITIONS OF ACCESS
By appointment.

PURPOSE OF ORGANIZATION
To serve the Hispanic Catholics in the Northeastern United States, from Maryland to Vermont. To provide support in the U.S. for the activities of the Catholic Church in Latin America.

ACTIVITIES/FIELDS OF RESEARCH
(1) Social doctrine of the Catholic Church; (2) Church/state relations; (3) Role of the Church in international and/or intergovernmental organizations; (4) The Catholic Church in the defense and promotion of human rights; (5) Hispanics in the U.S.

PUBLICATIONS
Presencia, a monthly newsletter.

PAN AMERICAN SOCIETY
680 Park Avenue
New York, NY 10021
(212) 744-6868

ORGANIZATIONAL STATUS
Nonprofit organization.

PARENTAL ORGANIZATION/AFFILIATION
The Americas Society.

MEMBERSHIP
Individual.

PURPOSE OF ORGANIZATION
The Pan American Society of the United States was organized in 1912 to promote friendly relations through improved understanding among the peoples of the American republics. It is the oldest such organization, and its members are individuals throughout the Americas interested in furthering the ideals and goal of Pan Americanism.

ACTIVITIES
Educational awards and honors for high school students, including those who have excelled in the study of the Spanish language. The Society also confers awards on presidents and private sector leaders in the hemisphere.

RESEARCH FACILITIES
Small collection of major literary works of the hemisphere, plus selection of works on Latin American Studies.

PUBLICATIONS
Annual Report (once a year); *Update* (bimonthly newsletter); *Calendar* (monthly listing of events).

PARLIAMENTARIANS GLOBAL ACTION
211 East 43rd Street, Suite 1604
New York, NY 10017
(212) 687-7755

ORGANIZATIONAL STATUS
Nongovernmental organization.

MEMBERSHIP
Members of internationally recognized national or supranational parliaments, or other forms of legislature, who are active on disarmament, development and peacekeeping issues.

PURPOSE OF ORGANIZATION
To promote world peace through enforceable world law for world citizens through parliamentary action; promote world order at the highest levels of government by using legislators to contact high ranking officials; demonstrate political support for measures to end the arms race and abolish the war system.

ACTIVITIES/FIELDS OF RESEARCH
Many members are elected legislators of Latin American parliaments: Argentina, Brazil, Peru, Uruguay, Costa Rica, Mexico. Interchange takes place with them on development issues and also on the linkage between military spending and the external debt. The group coordinates efforts on disarmament and development.

PUBLICATIONS
Global Action for Survival (annual); *Politicians for Peace* (annual); *Politics for Survival* (annual).

 THE POPULATION COUNCIL
One Dag Hammarskjold Plaza
New York, NY 10017
(212) 644-1300

ORGANIZATIONAL STATUS
International nonprofit organization.

PURPOSE OF ORGANIZATION

The Council works in three areas: (1) biomedical research in the field of human reproduction to develop and improve contraceptive methods, (2) social science research on the causes of population change, their societal implications and appropriate policy responses, and (3) provision of technical assistance to family planning and other population-related programs at local, national and regional levels. The Council produces publications for researchers, policymakers and the public and supports fellowships for advanced degree training.

ACTIVITIES/FIELDS OF RESEARCH

Operations research and evaluation in the area of family planning are conducted through a regional program begun in 1984. Additional collaborative activities are undertaken to promote better implementation of population policies and programs through technical assistance and the introduction of reversible birth control developed by the Council. The main areas of research within Latin America relate to the determinants of child health and mortality, adolescent fertility and enhancement of women's participation in development programs.

RESEARCH FACILITIES

The New York library contains an extensive international collection. Outside use of this facility is granted at the discretion of the librarian. Programs are managed by three regional Council offices in Bangkok, Cairo and Mexico City, and an interregional office in New York which is organized into four divisions (the Center for Biomedical Research, the Center for Policy Studies, International Programs and the Office of Communications). Technical assistance in Latin America is also provided by staff residents in Brazil, Colombia and Peru.

PUBLICATIONS

Population and Development Review (quarterly research journal); *Studies in Family Planning* (bimonthly research journal). New York staff provide direction for the above research journals which publish peer-reviewed articles, book reviews and documents. *Center for Policy Studies* and *International Programs Working Papers* (periodic distribution of selected staff research); *Center for Policy Studies Population Notes; NORPLANT®Worldwide* (three issues per year reporting on activities relating to the introduction of a Council-developed contraceptive); *Alternativas* (semiannual newsletter distributed by the Mexico City office, reporting on operations research and evaluation in the area of family planning conducted in Latin America); *Fertility Determinants Research Notes.*

RESEARCH INSTITUTE FOR THE STUDY OF MAN
162 East 78th Street
New York, NY 10021
(212) 535-8448

ORGANIZATIONAL STATUS
Nonprofit research center.

CONDITIONS OF ACCESS
Use of library facilities and consultation by appointment.

PURPOSE OF ORGANIZATION
Educational and scientific purposes. The Institute conducts research and training programs; supports scholarly exchanges and publications; organizes conferences; provides consultation services and stimulates the initiation, development and dissemination of basic knowledge in the behavioral sciences. Its primary geographical focus is on the Caribbean region.

FIELDS OF RESEARCH
Anthropology and behavioral sciences.

RESEARCH FACILITIES
Maintains a library of 15,000 publications and typescripts on the Caribbean as well as social anthropology.

SOCIAL SCIENCE RESEARCH COUNCIL
605 Third Avenue
New York, NY 10158
(212) 661-0280

ORGANIZATIONAL STATUS
Nonprofit research council.

PARENTAL ORGANIZATION/AFFILIATION
Affiliated with the American Council of Learned Societies.

PURPOSE OF ORGANIZATION
To further research in Latin American studies in a variety of ways: the appointment of a committee of scholars to set priorities and make plans for critical areas of research; the support of individual research through predoctoral fellowships and advanced research grants; the sponsorship of research conferences, often inter-

disciplinary and international; and the sponsorship of books and other research publications that may result from these activities.

ACTIVITIES/FIELDS OF RESEARCH
The Research Council's most recent planning activities include the following: The Culture of Fear; Political Economy of Health in Africa and Latin America; Popular Culture in Latin America; Popular Religion in Latin America; Gender Hierarchy; International Military Relations; Transition in Small, Peripheral Economies; Culture and Repression in Uruguay; Political Parties in the Southern Cone; Agrarian Production Relations; Caribbean Migration; Fertility Decline; Foreign Policy Alternatives in Central America.

PUBLICATIONS
The Council will furnish a publications list upon request.

SPANISH INSTITUTE
684 Park Avenue
New York, NY 10021
(212) 628-0420

93

ORGANIZATIONAL STATUS
Nonprofit organization.

MEMBERSHIP
Individuals, students, families, patrons, and corporations.

PURPOSE OF ORGANIZATION
To spread and promote Spanish culture in the U.S., namely its politics, economy, literature and art.

ACTIVITIES/FIELDS OF RESEARCH
Conferences and symposia on Spanish literature, history and politics are organized. The Institute has an art gallery. Spanish and Catalonian languages are taught at the Institute. An ESL program has been recently implemented.

RESEARCH FACILITIES
The Institute maintains a library , mostly of literary works from Spain. In addition, a collection of the most important newspapers, magazines and literary magazines is maintained.

PUBLICATIONS
Newsletter.

THE TINKER FOUNDATION INCORPORATED
55 East 59th Street
New York, NY 10022
(212) 421-6858

ORGANIZATIONAL STATUS
Private foundation.

PURPOSE OF ORGANIZATION
To support institutional projects focusing on the Spanish- and Portuguese-speaking countries in the Western Hemisphere as well as Portugal and Spain.

FIELDS OF RESEARCH
The Tinker Foundation is concerned with activities related to Ibero-America, Spain and Portugal. Priority is given to projects within the broad field of the social sciences with particular emphasis on areas such as international relations, urban and regional studies, education, communications management and economics. The Foundation also encourages projects on natural resource development, the training of specialists at the postgraduate level, and programs designed to further the education of Spanish-or Portuguese-speaking people of the United States.

PUBLICATIONS
Annual Report; Semiannual listing of Foundation-supported scholars and projects.

TWENTIETH CENTURY FUND
41 East 70th Street
New York, NY 10021
(212) 535-4441

ORGANIZATIONAL STATUS
Public policy research foundation.

PURPOSE OF ORGANIZATION
To support and supervise the research and writing of papers and books on policy issues.

ACTIVITIES/FIELDS OF RESEARCH
Economic development; debt crisis; U.S. policy toward Latin America; immigration policy, and others.

PUBLICATIONS
Fund papers and books appear periodically. Past titles include: *The Alliance that Lost its Way; U.S. Policy in the Caribbean; Multinationals in Latin America; The Role of Economic Advisors in Developing Countries; Puerto Rico: A Colonial Experiment.*

Projects in progress include: Fund papers on Costa Rica and on Brazil, as well as Fund books on Latin America debt and development, on the democratic revolution in Latin America, and on U.S.-Mexican relations.

UNIVERSITY OF THE LATIN AMERICAN WORKERS (UTAL)/ LATIN AMERICAN CONFEDERATION OF WORKERS (CLAT)
U.S. Office
Location: 34-48 70th Street, Jackson Heights, NY 11372
Mail: P.O. Box 39, Jackson Heights, NY 11372-0039
(718) 898-3600

ORGANIZATIONAL STATUS
Information and liaison office for the United States, United Nations and Canada.

PARENTAL ORGANIZATION/AFFILIATION
The U.S.O./CLAT is the official office of the UTAL/CLAT located in Caracas, Venezuela.

CONDITIONS OF ACCESS
Upon request our Center of Labor Information is available to researchers and others interested in Latin American/Caribbean labor issues.

PURPOSE OF ORGANIZATION
To promote greater interest and understanding of UTAL/CLAT and foster dialogue and cooperation; to provide information to those in the United States, Canada and the United Nations interested in UTAL/CLAT activities, publications and positions; to develop a labor library; to inform and orient UTAL/CLAT and others in Latin America and the Caribbean about U.S. activities, publications, conferences, etc., that could be of interest to them; to seek financial support for programs in Latin America.

ACTIVITIES/FIELDS OF RESEARCH
The Office sponsors or cosponsors conferences and seminars on labor-related

issues, in particular when labor leaders from CLAT or others travel to the U.S.A. Facilitation of contacts and dialogue between labor leaders from Latin America and the Caribbean with U.S. labor leaders and others interested in labor issues. Facilitation of activities of cooperatives and peasant organizations in the Americas.

RESEARCH FACILITIES
The Office has been developing, since 1979, a Center of Documentation of the Americas containing labor publications, books and newspaper articles.

PUBLICATIONS
(1) *CLAT Report:* A quarterly publication, 4 pp.; (2) *Informativo CLAT:* Official monthly publication of CLAT edited and published in Spanish by the Department of Social Communications from Caracas, Venezuela. (3) *CCT en Acción*: Bimonthly publication in Spanish edited in San José, Costa Rica with news on Central America. (4) Books are published in Spanish from Caracas, an average of four per year. Conference reports are mimeographed. A list of published books is available upon request. There are regular publications from many national affiliates of CLAT available upon request and by subscription.

WORLD JEWISH CONGRESS (WJC)
501 Madison Avenue, 17th Floor
New York, NY 10022
(212) 755-5770

ORGANIZATIONAL STATUS
Nonprofit organization.

PURPOSE OF ORGANIZATION
WJC is the representative body of Jewish communities around the world.

ACTIVITIES/FIELDS OF RESEARCH
The WJC research arm, the London-based Institute of Jewish Affairs, does extensive research into Jewish conditions throughout the world, including those of the Latin American countries.

RESEARCH FACILITIES
Central holdings are at the Institute of Jewish Affairs in London. WJC New York offices can secure material.

PUBLICATIONS
OJI, the biweekly publication in Spanish of the Latin American Jewish Congress (published in Buenos Aires), surveys events and activities of the Jewish communities of Latin America.

YIVO INSTITUTE FOR JEWISH RESEARCH
1048 Fifth Avenue
New York, NY 10028
(212) 535-6700

ORGANIZATIONAL STATUS
Professional/academic association.

PARENTAL ORGANIZATION/AFFILIATION
Independent organization.

MEMBERSHIP
General membership organization.

CONDITIONS OF ACCESS
Open to the public.

PURPOSE OF ORGANIZATION
The Institute's field of specialization is the history and culture of Ashkenazic Jewry, including Latin America and the Caribbean.

ACTIVITIES/FIELDS OF RESEARCH
Collecting materials pertinent to Jews in Latin America.

LIBRARY/RESEARCH FACILITIES
An academic library of 350,000 volumes is maintained, including manuscript collections.

PUBLICATIONS
Quarterly newsletter. Monographs are published occasionally.

CHAMBERS OF COMMERCE
AND GOVERNMENT OFFICES

The following information was requested for each entry in this section. However, final entries contain only those categories which each organization deemed applicable.

Identification:
- Name
- Address
- Telephone

Organizational status

Parental organization/affiliation

Conditions of Access

Membership

Purpose of organization

Activities/Fields of research

Research facilities

Publications

THE ARGENTINE-AMERICAN CHAMBER OF COMMERCE INC.

50 West 34th Street, 6th Floor, Room C-2
New York, NY 10001
(212) 564-3855

ORGANIZATIONAL STATUS
Nongovernmental organization.

MEMBERSHIP
Corporations, individuals, students.

PURPOSE OF ORGANIZATION
To promote and develop good business relations between the U.S. and Argentina, and to increase understanding and communication between both countries at the commercial, social and political levels.

ACTIVITIES/FIELDS OF RESEARCH
Symposia and conferences with the participation of business people and government officials from both countries are organized.

PUBLICATIONS
Bimonthly bulletin.

BRAZILIAN-AMERICAN CHAMBER OF COMMERCE, INC.

22 West 48th Street, Suite 404
New York, NY 10036
(212) 575-9030

ORGANIZATIONAL STATUS
Binational, private sector, nonprofit chamber of commerce.

MEMBERSHIP
300-350 members.

PURPOSE OF ORGANIZATION
To develop and promote an ever higher level of trade, investment and economic relations between Brazil and the United States.

ACTIVITIES/FIELDS OF RESEARCH
Brazil's economy and its foreign trade relations, particularly with the United States.

RESEARCH FACILITIES
The Berent Friele Library at the Chamber offers a wide selection of newspapers, magazines, economic reports, directories, newsletter series, bank and company reports, census data, guidelines, reference books and telephone directories pertinent to doing business with Brazil. Chamber files also deal with specific subject matter useful to researchers.

PUBLICATIONS
Brazilian-American Business Review/Directory (annual); *Brazilian-American Chamber of Commerce News Bulletin* (monthly); *Brazil-U.S. Business Listing* (irregular; last two editions were in 1980 and 1985).

CHAMBER OF COMMERCE OF LATIN AMERICA IN THE UNITED STATES
One World Trade Center, Suite 2343
New York, NY 10048-0231
(212) 432-9313

ORGANIZATIONAL STATUS
Nonprofit organization.

MEMBERSHIP
Individual and corporate.

PURPOSE OF ORGANIZATION
To promote international trade, especially exports from the U.S. to Latin America.

PUBLICATIONS
Inter-American Foreign Trade, quarterly news bulletin.

COLOMBIAN GOVERNMENT TRADE BUREAU
250 Park Avenue, 13th Floor
New York, NY 10177
(212) 972-7474

ORGANIZATIONAL STATUS
Commercial information and trade promotion office.

PARENTAL ORGANIZATION/ AFFILIATION
Export Promotion Fund, Prœxpo, Central Bank and Embassy of Colombia.

PURPOSE OF ORGANIZATION
To promote exports from Colombia to the United States and investment of U.S. firms in Colombia.

PUBLICATIONS
Exporters Directory (annual), and several publications on Colombia's economy.

COMMONWEALTH OF PUERTO RICO
304 Park Avenue South
New York, NY 10010
(212) 260-3000

ORGANIZATIONAL STATUS
Government agency.

PURPOSE OF ORGANIZATION
To render services and assistance to the Hispanic community, in general, and the Puerto Rican community, in particular. Services include education, employment, ID documentation, organization of community groups, etc.

ACTIVITIES/FIELDS OF RESEARCH
Study and research unit. Comparisons of Puerto Rican migrant movement, degree of education, member of English speaking migrants comparison with unemployment information of other groups, etc.

PUBLICATIONS
Agency production; Monthly reports; Information communiqués for media.

CORPORACION DE FOMENTO
DE LA PRODUCCION (CORFO)
New York Office
One World Trade Center, Suite 5151
New York, NY 10048-0497
(212) 938-0550

ORGANIZATIONAL STATUS
Autonomous instrumentality of the Government of Chile.

PURPOSE OF ORGANIZATION
To help in the country's economic development by granting loans and technical assistance for basic projects and national programs in new areas or helping those in the private sector to improve and grow.

FUNCTIONS/PROGRAMS/RESEARCH ACTIVITIES
CORFO has put special emphasis on the execution of specific projects of applied investigation, both in technological subjects and exploration and evaluation of the potential natural and productive resources of the country. CORFO's nine research institutes specialize in the fields of mining, technology, fisheries, forestry and professional training.

RESEARCH FACILITIES
A small reference library is maintained.

PUBLICATIONS
Chile Economic Report (monthly).

  ### ECUADOREAN GOVERNMENT TRADE OFFICE
757 Third Avenue, Suite 17B
New York, NY 10017
(212) 688-6858

ORGANIZATIONAL STATUS
Foreign government office.

PARENTAL ORGANIZATION/AFFILIATION
Ministry of Industry, Commerce, Integration and Fishery, Ecuador.

PURPOSE OF ORGANIZATION
To market Ecuadorean products, to promote foreign investment in Ecuador and to guide American businesspersons trading with Ecuador.

PUBLICATIONS
Invest in Ecuador and *Import and Export Regulations* (these publications are updated whenever the government issues new regulations); tourist information and general information.

FEDERAL RESERVE BANK OF NEW YORK
33 Liberty Street
New York, NY 10045
(212) 720-5000

106

ACTIVITIES/FIELDS OF RESEARCH
Research activities are developed by various groups, such as the Research and Statistics Group and the International Research Department. Some studies are published, including Latin American and Caribbean issues.

Call Public Information Department:
(212) 720-6130.

PUBLICATIONS
Publications available cover topics such as the *Federal Reserve System, Financial Markets and Instruments, Money and Banking,* and *International Topics.*

One copy of both the *Quarterly Review* and the *Annual Report* are sent free to subscribers and multiple copies may also be purchased.

GOVERNOR'S OFFICE FOR HISPANIC AFFAIRS
2 World Trade Center, 57th Floor, Suite 5777
New York, NY 10047
(212) 587-2266

107

ORGANIZATIONAL STATUS
Executive Chamber of Governor's Office.

PARENTAL ORGANIZATION/AFFILIATION
Governor's Office.

PURPOSE OF ORGANIZATION
To develop and increase opportunities for involvement and employment of Hispanics in all aspects of state government; to provide information and assistance in the development of policies which will improve the quality of life of Hispanics; to develop opportunities for business enterprises owned by Hispanics to participate in state contracts; to act as advocate for the Hispanic community; to coordinate, when necessary, special projects, and special studies and evaluations.

PUBLICATIONS
Newsletter.

THE INVESTMENT COUNCIL OF PANAMA
2586 Riverside Drive
Wantagh, NY 11793
(516) 781-1864

ORGANIZATIONAL STATUS
Foreign government office.

PURPOSE OF ORGANIZATION
To promote investment in Panama; to identify areas of interest to investors and to encourage economic development through private initiative.

PUBLICATIONS
Literature on Panamanian trade, corporations, industry and manufactures, service industry, banking and reinsurance is available upon request.

THE MEXICAN CHAMBER OF COMMERCE OF THE UNITED STATES, INC.
15 Park Row
New York, NY 10038
(212) 227-9171

ORGANIZATIONAL STATUS
International chamber of commerce.

CONDITIONS OF ACCESS
By application.

PURPOSE OF ORGANIZATION
To promote industry and trade between Mexico and the United States as it affects the membership. To provide services and facilities to its members to further their businesses.

ACTIVITIES/FIELDS OF RESEARCH
Periodic meetings and seminars covering a wide range of subjects in the fields of exports, imports, trade relations, investments, tourism, etc. Research limited to specific inquiries from members.

RESEARCH FACILITIES
Reference library available to members contains trade directories, Mexican newspapers and magazines, trade journals, economic reports, official government publications, Mexican telephone books, industry reports, trade statistics, etc.

PUBLICATIONS
Monthly Digest; Membership Directory (no specific publication date).

NEW YORK STATE HISPANIC CHAMBER OF COMMERCE   110
210 East 86th Street, Suite 502A
New York, NY 10028
(212) 737-9708

CONDITIONS OF ACCESS
Membership; request for information.

PURPOSE OF ORGANIZATION
To help and represent Hispanic business interests to join mainstream American business community.

ACTIVITIES/FIELDS OF RESEARCH
Activities include conferences, seminars and periodic publications; also annual banquet awards ceremonies, monthly meetings, etc.

RESEARCH FACILITIES
The Chamber of Commerce has a small but adequate library which catalogues the latest items of concern to its members, e.g. small business development; financing; economic development issues, including Latin America and the Caribbean.

PUBLICATIONS
Monthly newsletter and important bulletin reports.

NORTH AMERICAN-CHILEAN CHAMBER OF COMMERCE, INC.   111
220 East 81st Street
New York, NY 10028
(212) 288-5691

ORGANIZATIONAL STATUS
Nonprofit organization.

MEMBERSHIP
Individual and corporate.

PURPOSE OF ORGANIZATION
To promote and expand trade and commercial relations between the U.S. and Chile; to provide a forum for leading Chilean, Canadian and American industrialists, economists, bankers and financial executives to exchange information on issues of their immediate interest.

PUBLICATIONS
Pertinent materials gathered from government reports and from business and technical publications are distributed to members.

PERU-COMMERCIAL OFFICE
747 Third Avenue, 28th Floor
New York, NY 10017
(212) 688-9110

ORGANIZATIONAL STATUS
Foreign government office.

PARENTAL ORGANIZATION/AFFILIATION
Instituto de Comercio Exterior (state agency).

PURPOSE OF ORGANIZATION
To promote mainly nontraditional Peruvian exports.

FUNCTIONS/PROGRAMS/RESEARCH ACTIVITIES
Market studies for Peruvian products; maintaining and expanding relations between importers and exporters from the U.S. and Peru.

RESEARCH FACILITIES
A small library is maintained.

PUBLICATIONS
Monthly economic report.

PORT AUTHORITY OF NEW YORK AND NEW JERSEY
World Trade Institute
One World Trade Center, 55th Floor
New York, NY 10048
(212) 466-8278

ACTIVITIES/FIELDS OF RESEARCH
The Port Authority maintains, monitors and analyzes foreign trade between the New York/New Jersey region and the world. This includes Latin America and the Caribbean. It provides courses at the World Trade Institute on international trade transactions with various countries, including those of Latin America and the Caribbean. The World Trade Institute Language School has scheduled courses in Spanish and Portuguese.

RESEARCH FACILITIES
The library is located at: *One World Trade Center, 55th Floor.*
For information, call: *(212) 466-4067.*

PUERTO RICO CHAMBER OF COMMERCE IN THE U.S., INC.
102 West 79th Street
New York, NY 10024
(212) 724-4731

ORGANIZATIONAL STATUS
Nonprofit association.

MEMBERSHIP
Members must be companies based in the continental U.S. with branches in Puerto Rico.

PURPOSE OF ORGANIZATION
To help U.S. corporations with legislation in Washington D.C. and Puerto Rico.

ACTIVITIES/FIELDS OF RESEARCH
Seminars are offered throughout the year in the area of Puerto Rican business and economy.

PUBLICATIONS
Monthly newsletter; acts of law, as they are passed; information on Puerto Rico.

 URUGUAYAN GOVERNMENT TRADE BUREAU
747 Third Avenue, 37th Floor
New York, NY 10017
(212) 751-7137/7138

ORGANIZATIONAL STATUS
Government office.

PARENTAL ORGANIZATION/AFFILIATION
Ministry of Economy of Uruguay.

PURPOSE OF ORGANIZATION
To promote trade and investment flows between Uruguay and the U.S., especially Uruguayan exports and U.S. investment.

ACTIVITIES/FIELDS OF RESEARCH
Market research and market reports at the request of private sector organizations (U.S. importers) or the Dirección General de Comercio Exterior.

LATIN AMERICAN
AND CARIBBEAN CONSULATES
AND MISSIONS TO THE UNITED NATIONS

The following information was requested for each entry in this section. However, final entries contain only those categories which each organization deemed applicable.

Identification:
  - Name
  - Address
  - Telephone

Hours of Service

Libraries and reference facilities

Publications

Sponsored events and programs

CONSULATES

CONSULATE GENERAL OF ARGENTINA
12 West 56th Street
New York, NY 10019
(212) 603-0400

116

HOURS OF SERVICE
9:00 a.m. to 1:30 p.m., Monday through Friday.

LIBRARIES/REFERENCE FACILITIES
9:00 a.m. to 4:00 p.m., Monday through Friday, by appointment only.

SPONSORED EVENTS AND PROGRAMS
Exhibitions (painting, sculpture, arts and crafts); seminars, lectures, concerts (piano, guitar, etc.); workshops; theater; individual projects.

CONSULATE GENERAL OF THE BAHAMAS
767 Third Avenue
New York, NY 10017
(212) 421-6420

117

HOURS OF SERVICE
Public admission: 10:00 a.m. to 4:00 p.m., Monday through Friday.

LIBRARIES/REFERENCE FACILITIES
Reading room.

PUBLICATIONS
Law books, Central Bank quarterlies, general investment, budget communications, and general information.

CONSULATE GENERAL OF BARBADOS
800 Second Avenue
New York, NY 10017
(212) 867-8435

118

HOURS OF SERVICE
10:00 a.m. to 3:00 p.m., Monday through Friday.

CONSULATE GENERAL OF BOLIVIA
211 East 43rd Street, Suite 802
New York, NY 10017
(212) 687-0530

HOURS OF SERVICE
10:00 a.m. to 4:00 p.m., Monday through Friday.

CONSULATE GENERAL OF BRAZIL
630 Fifth Avenue
New York, NY 10111
(212) 757-3080

HOURS OF SERVICE
9:30 a.m. to 3:30 p.m., Monday through Friday.

LIBRARIES/REFERENCE FACILITIES
A library is maintained.

PUBLICATIONS
Calendar of events.

SPONSORED EVENTS AND PROGRAMS
Occasional events are sponsored.

CONSULATE GENERAL OF CHILE
866 United Nations Plaza, Room 302
New York, NY 10017
(212) 980-3366

HOURS OF SERVICE
9:00 a.m. to 1:00 p.m., Monday through Friday.

LIBRARIES/REFERENCE FACILITIES
A small library is maintained.

PUBLICATIONS
Chile Today, monthly (summary of recent events in Chile).

SPONSORED EVENTS AND PROGRAMS
Occasional exhibits are organized by the Chilean Trade Office "Pro-Chile".

CONSULATE GENERAL OF COLOMBIA
10 East 46th Street
New York, NY 10017
(212) 949-9898

HOURS OF SERVICE
9:00 a.m. to 2:00 p.m., Monday through Friday.

LIBRARIES/REFERENCE FACILITIES
At the *Colombian Information Service, 140 East 57th Street New York, NY 10022 (212) 421-8270.*

PUBLICATIONS
Tourist information at the *Colombian Center, 140 East 57th Street, 2nd Floor, New York, NY 10022 (212) 688-0151.*

CONSULATE GENERAL OF THE COMMONWEALTH OF DOMINICA
89-18 191st Street
Hollis, NY 11423
(718) 468-4811

HOURS OF SERVICE
By appointment, 10:00 a.m. to 6:00 p.m., Monday through Friday.

CONSULATE GENERAL OF COSTA RICA
80 Wall Street, Suite 1117
New York, NY 10005
(212) 425-2620

HOURS OF SERVICE
9:00 a.m. to 2:00 p.m., Monday through Friday.

CONSULATE GENERAL OF THE DOMINICAN REPUBLIC
17 West 60th Street
New York, NY 10023
(212) 265-0630

HOURS OF SERVICE
9:30 a.m. to 3:00 p.m., Monday through Friday; 9:30 a.m. to 1:00 p.m., Saturday.

CONSULATE GENERAL OF ECUADOR
18 East 41st Street
New York, NY 10017
(212) 683-7555

HOURS OF SERVICE
9:00 a.m. to 2:00 p.m., Monday through Friday.

CONSULATE GENERAL OF EL SALVADOR
46 Park Avenue
New York, NY 10016
(212) 889-3608

HOURS OF SERVICE
9:30 a.m. to 3:00 p.m., Monday through Friday.

CONSULATE GENERAL OF GRENADA
820 Second Avenue, Suite 1100
New York, NY 10017
(212) 599-0301

HOURS OF SERVICE
10:00 a.m. to 3:30 p.m., Monday through Friday.

CONSULATE GENERAL OF GUATEMALA
57 Park Avenue
New York, NY 10016
(212) 686-3837

HOURS OF SERVICE
9:30 a.m. to 12:30 p.m., Monday through Friday.

LIBRARIES/REFERENCE FACILITIES
Newspapers and other Guatemalan publications are available for consultation.

PUBLICATIONS
Brochures and pamphlets are available.

CONSULATE GENERAL OF GUYANA
622 Third Avenue, 35th Floor
New York, NY 10017
(212) 953-0920

130

HOURS OF SERVICE
9:30 a.m. to 4:00 p.m., Monday through Friday.

CONSULATE GENERAL OF HAITI
60 East 42nd Street
New York, NY 10017
(212) 697-9767

131

HOURS OF SERVICE
9:30 a.m. to 3:45 p.m., Monday through Friday; 10:00 a.m. to 3:00 p.m., Saturday.

CONSULATE GENERAL OF HONDURAS
18 East 41st Street
New York, NY 10017
(212) 889-3858

132

HOURS OF SERVICE
9:30 a.m. to 3:00 p.m., Monday through Friday.

LIBRARIES/REFERENCE FACILITIES
Honduran publications are available for consultation.

CONSULATE GENERAL OF JAMAICA
866 Second Avenue
New York, NY 10017-2993
(212) 935-9000

133

HOURS OF SERVICE
9:00 a.m. to 5:00 p.m., Monday through Friday.

LIBRARIES/REFERENCE FACILITIES
A number of Jamaican publications are available for research purposes, e.g., laws of Jamaica, culture, history and economics.

PUBLICATIONS
A weekly summary of news from Jamaica is available. From time to time, releases on particular events are issued.

SPONSORED EVENTS AND PROGRAMS
An annual service of Thanksgiving is held on the Sunday before the first Monday in August, in honor of Jamaica's independence. Events are held celebrating Jamaica's National Heritage Week (third week in October).

 CONSULATE GENERAL OF MEXICO
8 East 41st Street
New York, NY 10017
(212) 689-0456

HOURS OF SERVICE
9:00 a.m. to 2:00 p.m., 3:00 p.m. to 5:00 p.m.. Monday through Friday.

LIBRARIES/REFERENCE FACILITIES
Texts, documents and general information on Mexican matters are available for consultation.

PUBLICATIONS
Commercial information: (212) 759-9502; tourist information: (212) 838-2949.

SPONSORED EVENTS AND PROGRAMS
Mexican art gallery sponsors lectures, painting and sculpture exhibitions and films.

 CONSULATE GENERAL OF PANAMA
1270 Avenue of the Americas, Suite 408
New York, NY 10020
(212) 246-3771/3772

HOURS OF SERVICE
9:00 a.m. to 3:30 p.m., Monday through Friday.

 CONSULATE GENERAL OF PARAGUAY
One World Trade Center
New York, NY 10048
(212) 432-0733

HOURS OF SERVICE
10:00 a.m. to 2:00 p.m., Monday through Friday.

CONSULATE GENERAL OF PERU
805 Third Avenue, 14th Floor
New York, NY 10022
(212) 644-2850

HOURS OF SERVICE
9:00 a.m. to 5:00 p.m., Monday through Friday.

PUBLICATIONS
The Consulate has a great deal of information regarding economic, commercial, cultural and touristic development in Peru.

SPONSORED EVENTS AND PROGRAMS
Events to promote Peruvian culture and art are organized.

CONSULATE GENERAL OF THE REPUBLIC OF TRINIDAD AND TOBAGO
420 Lexington Avenue, Room 333
New York, NY 10017
(212) 682-7272

HOURS OF SERVICE
9:30 a.m. to 3:30 p.m., Monday through Friday.

LIBRARIES/REFERENCE FACILITIES
Limited facilities. Publications may be used on premises; no borrowing is allowed.

PUBLICATIONS
Most Trinidad and Tobago Government publications are available at the Consulate.

CONSULATE GENERAL OF ST. KITTS AND NEVIS

414 East 75th Street
New York, NY 10021
(212) 535-1234

HOURS OF SERVICE
9:00 a.m. to 5:00 p.m., Monday through Friday.

CONSULATE GENERAL OF SAINT LUCIA
41 East 42nd Street
New York, NY 10017
(212) 697-9361

HOURS OF SERVICE
9:00 a.m. to 5:00 p.m., Monday through Friday.

LIBRARIES/REFERENCE FACILITIES
Reference material on Saint Lucia and Eastern Caribbean is available for consultation. Restrictive loan policy.

PUBLICATIONS
Economic, social and political data on Saint Lucia.

SPONSORED EVENTS AND PROGRAMS
Group lectures by request.

CONSULATE GENERAL OF
ST. VINCENT AND THE GRENADINES
801 Second Avenue
New York, NY 10017
(212) 687-4490

HOURS OF SERVICE
9:00 a.m. to 5:00 p.m., Monday through Friday.

LIBRARIES/REFERENCE FACILITIES
A consultation library is maintained.

PUBLICATIONS
Publications from and dealing with St.Vincent and the Grenadines, in addition to UN publications, are available for consultation.

CONSULATE GENERAL OF URUGUAY
747 Third Avenue
New York, NY 10017
(212) 753-8191

HOURS OF SERVICE
9:00 a.m. to 3:00 p.m., Monday through Friday.

PUBLICATIONS
Monthly Cultural calendar.

SPONSORED EVENTS AND PROGRAMS
Art exhibits, conferences, singers.

CONSULATE GENERAL OF VENEZUELA
7 East 51st Street
New York, NY 10022
(212) 826-1660

HOURS OF SERVICE
9:00 a.m. to 4:00 p.m., Monday through Friday.

LIBRARIES/REFERENCE FACILITIES
Information on imports/exports, as well as on other subjects related to different
fields in Venezuela, is available at the Public Relations Department.

SPONSORED EVENTS AND PROGRAMS
Permanent exhibit of Venezuelan works of art at the *Galeria Venezuela* located at
the Consulate. For information on the exhibits, call *(212) 826-1680.*

MISSIONS TO THE UNITED NATIONS

PERMANENT MISSION OF ARGENTINA
TO THE UNITED NATIONS
One United Nations Plaza, 25th Floor
New York, NY 10017
(212) 688-6300

HOURS OF SERVICE
9:00 a.m. to 5:00 p.m., Monday through Friday; by appointment only.

LIBRARIES/REFERENCE FACILITIES
The Mission maintains a small library with United Nations publications, as well as
some Argentine books on matters concerning foreign relations.

PERMANENT MISSION OF THE COMMONWEALTH OF THE BAHAMAS TO THE UNITED NATIONS
767 Third Avenue, 9th Floor
New York, NY 10017
(212) 421-6925

HOURS OF SERVICE
9:00 a.m. to 5:00 p.m., Monday through Friday.

PERMANENT MISSION OF BARBADOS TO THE UNITED NATIONS
800 Second Avenue, 18th Floor
New York, NY 10017
(212) 867-8431

HOURS OF SERVICE
9:00 a.m. to 5:00 p.m., Monday through Friday.

LIBRARIES/REFERENCE FACILITIES
Economic and financial reports, newspapers, periodicals and official gazettes are available for consultation.

PERMANENT MISSION OF BELIZE TO THE UNITED NATIONS
801 Second Avenue, Suite 401
New York, NY 10017
(212) 599-0233/0286

HOURS OF SERVICE
9:00 a.m. to 5:00 p.m., Monday through Friday.

LIBRARIES/REFERENCE FACILITIES
Information on Belize is available on request.

PUBLICATIONS
Addresses to the UN General Assembly; *The New Belize* (monthly magazine); *Belize External Trade* (quarterly publication); *Belize Consumer Price Index;* budget speeches; information bulletins.

PERMANENT MISSION OF BOLIVIA
TO THE UNITED NATIONS
211 East 43rd Street
New York, NY 10017
(212) 682-8132

HOURS OF SERVICE
9:30 a.m. to 5:30 p.m., Monday through Friday.

LIBRARIES/REFERENCE FACILITIES
Newspapers, economic bulletins, IMF, World Bank and UN documents are available for consultation.

SPONSORED EVENTS AND PROGRAMS
Cultural events are sponsored occasionally .

PERMANENT MISSION OF BRAZIL
TO THE UNITED NATIONS
747 Third Avenue, 9th Floor
New York, NY 10017
(212) 832- 6868

HOURS OF SERVICE
9:00 a.m. to 7:00 p.m., Monday through Friday.

PUBLICATIONS
United Nations documents and publications; speeches made by Brazilian delegates to the United Nations.

PERMANENT MISSION OF CHILE
TO THE UNITED NATIONS
809 United Nations Plaza
New York, NY 10017
(212) 687-7547

HOURS OF SERVICE
9:00 a.m. to 6:00 p.m., Monday through Friday.

LIBRARIES/REFERENCE FACILITIES
A library is maintained including newspapers, magazines, reports and bulletins. Also government and UN documents are available.

SPONSORED EVENTS AND PROGRAMS
Cultural events are sponsored occasionally.

**PERMANENT MISSION OF COLOMBIA
TO THE UNITED NATIONS**
140 East 57th Street, 5th Floor
New York, NY 10022
(212) 355-7776/7777/7778

HOURS OF SERVICE
9:30 a.m. to 5:30 p.m., Monday through Friday.

LIBRARIES/REFERENCE FACILITIES
UN archives are available for consultation.

**PERMANENT MISSION
OF THE COMMONWEALTH
OF DOMINICA TO THE UNITED NATIONS**
Contact:
(212) 791-1872

**PERMANENT MISSION OF COSTA RICA
TO THE UNITED NATIONS**
211 East 43rd Street
New York, NY 10017
(212) 986-6373

HOURS OF SERVICE
10:00 a.m. to 6:00 p.m., Monday through Friday.

SPONSORED EVENTS AND PROGRAMS
Cultural events are sponsored occasionally.

**PERMANENT MISSION OF CUBA
TO THE UNITED NATIONS**
315 Lexington Avenue
New York, NY 10016
(212) 689-7215

HOURS OF SERVICE
9:00 a.m. to 1:00 p.m., 2:00 p.m. to 6:00 p.m., Monday through Friday.

PERMANENT MISSION
OF THE DOMINICAN REPUBLIC
TO THE UNITED NATIONS
144 East 44th Street, 4th Floor
New York, NY 10017
(212) 867-0833

HOURS OF SERVICE
9:00 a.m. to 4:00 p.m., Monday through Friday.

PERMANENT MISSION OF ECUADOR
TO THE UNITED NATIONS
820 Second Avenue, Room 1500
New York, NY 10017
(212) 986-6670

HOURS OF SERVICE
9:00 a.m. to 5:00 p.m., Monday through Friday.

PERMANENT MISSION OF EL SALVADOR
TO THE UNITED NATIONS
46 Park Avenue
New York, NY 10016
(212) 679-1616

HOURS OF SERVICE
9:30 a.m. to 5:00 p.m., Monday through Friday.

PERMANENT MISSION OF GRENADA
TO THE UNITED NATIONS
820 Second Avenue, 11th Floor
New York, NY 10017
(212) 599-0301

HOURS OF SERVICE
9:00 a.m. to 5:00 p.m., Monday through Friday.

LIBRARIES/REFERENCE FACILITIES
Publications dealing with Grenada are available.

PERMANENT MISSION OF GUATEMALA
TO THE UNITED NATIONS
57 Park Avenue
New York, NY 10016
(212) 679-4760/4761

HOURS OF SERVICE
9:30 a.m. to 5:30 p.m., Monday through Friday.

LIBRARIES/REFERENCE FACILITIES
Documents related to the participation of Guatemala as a member of the United Nations and information on Guatemala are available.

PUBLICATIONS
Statements from the Government or Ministry of Foreign Affairs of Guatemala before the General Assembly of the United Nations are published.

PERMANENT MISSION OF GUYANA
TO THE UNITED NATIONS
622 Third Avenue, 35th Floor
New York, NY 10017
(212) 953-0930

HOURS OF SERVICE
9:30 a.m. to 4:30 p.m., Monday through Friday.

PERMANENT MISSION OF HAITI
TO THE UNITED NATIONS
801 Second Avenue
New York, NY 10017
(212) 370-4840

HOURS OF SERVICE
9:30 a.m. to 5:30 p.m., Monday through Friday.

PERMANENT MISSION OF HONDURAS
TO THE UNITED NATIONS
866 United Nations Plaza
New York, NY 10017
(212) 752-3370

HOURS OF SERVICE
9:30 a.m. to 4:00 p.m., Monday through Friday.

LIBRARIES/REFERENCE FACILITIES
Documents and publications available for consultation by appointment only.

PERMANENT MISSION OF JAMAICA
TO THE UNITED NATIONS
866 Second Avenue, 15th Floor
New York, NY 10017
(212) 688-7040

HOURS OF SERVICE
9:00 a.m. to 5:00 p.m., Monday through Friday.

PERMANENT MISSION OF MEXICO
TO THE UNITED NATIONS
2 United Nations Plaza, 28th Floor
New York, NY 10017
(212) 752-0220

HOURS OF SERVICE
9:00 a.m. to 6:00 p.m., Monday through Friday.

LIBRARIES/REFERENCE FACILITIES
Documents available for consultation by appointment only.

SPONSORED EVENTS AND PROGRAMS
Cultural events and conferences are organized.

PERMANENT MISSION OF NICARAGUA TO THE UNITED NATIONS
820 Second Avenue
New York, NY 10017
(212) 490-7997

HOURS OF SERVICE
9:00 a.m. to 5:00 p.m., Monday through Friday.

LIBRARIES/REFERENCE FACILITIES
Pamphlets and updated information on Nicaraguan events are available upon request.

 PERMANENT MISSION OF PANAMA TO THE UNITED NATIONS
866 United Nations Plaza, Room 544
New York, NY 10017
(212) 421-5420

HOURS OF SERVICE
9:00 a.m. to 5:00 p.m., Monday through Friday.

LIBRARIES/REFERENCE FACILITIES
UN documents/archives pertaining to Panama are available for consultation by appointment only.

 PERMANENT MISSION OF PARAGUAY TO THE UNITED NATIONS
211 East 43rd Street
New York, NY 10017
(212) 687-3490

HOURS OF SERVICE
9:30 a.m. to 4:00 p.m., Monday through Friday.

PERMANENT MISSION OF PERU
TO THE UNITED NATIONS
820 Second Avenue
New York, NY 10017
(212) 687-3336

HOURS OF SERVICE
9:00 a.m. to 6:00 p.m., Monday through Friday.

PERMANENT MISSION OF THE REPUBLIC
OF TRINIDAD AND TOBAGO
TO THE UNITED NATIONS
675 Third Avenue, Suite 2201
New York, NY 10012
(212) 697-7620

HOURS OF SERVICE
9:00 a.m. to 5:00 p.m., Monday through Friday.

PERMANENT MISSION OF ST. KITTS AND NEVIS
TO THE UNITED NATIONS
414 East 75th Street
New York, NY 10021
(212) 535-1234

HOURS OF SERVICE
9:00 a.m. to 5:00 p.m., Monday through Friday.

PERMANENT MISSION OF SAINT LUCIA
TO THE UNITED NATIONS
41 East 42nd Street, Suite 315
New York, NY 10017
(212) 679-9360

HOURS OF SERVICE
9:00 a.m. to 5:00 p.m., Monday through Friday.

SPONSORED EVENTS AND PROGRAMS
Occasional lectures on Saint Lucia.

**PERMANENT MISSION
OF ST.VINCENT AND THE GRENADINES
TO THE UNITED NATIONS**
*801 Second Avenue, 21st Floor
New York, NY 10017
(212) 687-4490*

HOURS OF SERVICE
9:00 a.m. to 5:00 p.m., Monday through Friday.

**PERMANENT MISSION OF SURINAME
TO THE UNITED NATIONS**
*One United Nations Plaza
New York, NY 10017
(212) 826-0660*

HOURS OF SERVICE
9:00 a.m. to 5:00 p.m., Monday through Friday.

**PERMANENT MISSION OF URUGUAY
TO THE UNITED NATIONS**
*747 Third Avenue
New York, NY 10017
(212) 752-8240*

HOURS OF SERVICE
9:00 a.m. to 5:00 p.m., Monday through Friday.

**PERMANENT MISSION OF VENEZUELA
TO THE UNITED NATIONS**
*231 East 46th Street
New York, NY 10010
(212) 838-2800*

HOURS OF SERVICE
Winter hours: 9:00 a.m. to 1:00 p.m., 3:00 p.m. to 6:00 p.m., Monday through Friday; summer hours: 9:00 a.m. to 3:00 p.m., Monday through Friday.

LIBRARIES

The following information was requested for each entry in this section. However, final entries contain only those categories which each organization deemed applicable.

Identification:
- Name
- Address
- Telephone

General Information:
- Hours of service
- Conditions of access
- Cooperative arrangements with other institutions
- Facilities
- Special services for the handicapped

Size of collections and holdings:
- General holdings
- Holdings pertaining to Latin America

Description and evaluation of collection pertaining to Latin America:
- Description
- Evaluation of collection strength by subject and area category

Description of evaluation codes*:

Code	Description

A   *Basic level.* This level describes a highly selective collection, including introductory, background, and basic reference material, that serve to introduce and define the subject and to indicate the varieties of information available elsewhere. It includes major dictionaries and encyclopedias, selected editions of important works, historical surveys, important bibliographies, and a few major periodicals.

B   *Study level: MA and Undergraduate.* This level is intended to support undergraduate or graduate course work, or sustained independent study, i.e., which is adequate to maintain knowledge of a subject required for limited or generalized purposes or less than research intensity. It includes a wide range of basic monographs, complete collections of the works of important writers, a selection of representative journals, and the reference tools and fundamental bibliographical apparatus pertaining to the subject.

C   *Research level.* This level is intended to support ongoing research or likely future research leading to the Ph.D. It includes the major published source materials required for dissertations and independent research, all important reference works and a wide selection of specialized monograph and other secondary literature, as well as an extensive collection of journals.

D   *Advanced research level.* This level is intended to support doctoral and post- doctoral research with a high degree of adequacy. In addition to printed and microfilm material, it may include manuscripts and other special materials if they are appropriate and within the library's financial capabilities. It allows for indefinite expansion of the research program both at the level of faculty and postdoctoral, and Ph.D. research.

E   *Intensive level.* This selection level describes the effort to acquire so far as reasonable all available significant works of recorded knowledge for a necessarily defined and limited field, i.e., an intensive effort to acquire manuscript, archival and ephemeral material, etc., in addition to published sources. This level maintains or creates a special collection; the aim, if not the achievement, is exhaustiveness.

---

* From the Research Libraries Group.

List of subject categories covered:

1. Bibliography & Reference
2. Economics
3. Education
4. Geography & Anthropology
5. History
6. International Relations
7. Language & Literature
8. Law
9. Military Affairs
10. Philosophy & Religion
11. Politics & Government
12. Sociology

List of area categories covered:

13. Argentina
14. Belize
15. Bolivia
16. Brazil
17. Caribbean (excl. Cuba)
18. Chile
19. Colombia
20. Costa Rica
21. Cuba
22. Dominican Republic
23. Ecuador
24. El Salvador
25. Guatemala
26. Guianas
27. Haiti
28. Honduras
29. Jamaica
30. Mexico
31. Nicaragua
32. Panama
33. Paraguay
34. Peru
35. Uruguay
36. Venezuela
37. Other

Special collections:
- Government documents
- Miscellaneous vertical files
- Archives and Manuscripts
- Films and tapes
- Prominent collections, rare books, etc.

The following acronyms appear throughout this section:

CRL	Center for Research Libraries
LAMP	Latin American Microfilm Group
METRO	New York Metropolitan Reference and Research Library Agency
NJALN	New Jersey Academic Library Network
NYSILL	New York State Inter Library Loan
OCLC	On-Line Computer Center Inc.
RLG	Research Libraries Group

ARCHIBALD S. ALEXANDER LIBRARY
Rutgers, The State University of New Jersey
College Avenue at Huntington Street
New Brunswick, NJ 08903
(201) 932-7507

176

GENERAL INFORMATION

HOURS OF SERVICE
8:00 a.m. to 10:00 p.m., Monday through Thursday; 8:00 a.m. to 6:00 p.m., Friday; 12:00 noon to 10:00 p.m., Saturday; for summer hours and intersession hours, please call.

CONDITIONS OF ACCESS
Open to the public. Checking out restricted to students, faculty, staff and alumni.

COOPERATIVE ARRANGEMENTS WITH OTHER INSTITUTIONS
METRO; RLG; member of CRL.

FACILITIES
Computers, microreaders, reproduction equipment.

SPECIAL SERVICES FOR THE HANDICAPPED
Kurtzweil reading machine; special provisions for the handicapped.

SIZE OF COLLECTIONS/HOLDINGS

LATIN AMERICAN
35,000 volumes.

DESCRIPTION AND EVALUATION OF COLLECTION

LATIN AMERICAN HOLDINGS
The collection maintained by the Library includes the social sciences and 19th and 20th century literature.

EVALUATION OF
SUBJECT/AREA STRENGTH

Refer to page 110 for definitions
of collection rating levels.

Subject Category		Collection Rating Level (A-E) Monographs
1.	Bibliography & Reference	C
2.	Economics	C
3.	Education	B
4.	Geography & Anthropology	C
5.	History	C
6.	International Relations	C
7.	Language & Literature	C
8.	Law	-
9.	Military Affairs	B
10.	Philosophy & Religion	B
11.	Politics & Government	C
12.	Sociology	C

Area Category		Monographs
13.	Argentina	C
14.	Belize	-
15.	Bolivia	-
16.	Brazil	C
17.	Caribbean (excl. Cuba)	-
18.	Chile	B
19.	Colombia	-
20.	Costa Rica	-
21.	Cuba	-
22.	Dominican Republic	-
23.	Ecuador	-
24.	El Salvador	-
25.	Guatemala	-
26.	Guianas	-
27.	Haiti	-
28.	Honduras	-
29.	Jamaica	-
30.	Mexico	C
31.	Nicaragua	-
32.	Panama	-
33.	Paraguay	-
34.	Peru	-
35.	Uruguay	-
36.	Venezuela	-
37.	Other	-

SPECIAL COLLECTIONS

GOVERNMENT DOCUMENTS
Partial census from Argentina, Brazil, and Mexico. Fair collection of Diarios de Sesiones (Congressional sessions) and Census of Buenos Aires-Argentina. Annual reports from Central Banks of various countries.

ARCHIVES AND MANUSCRIPTS
Manuscripts by R. J. Alexander on interviews: Latin American Politics (1960s and 1970s). Frances Grant manuscripts from the 1940s.

FILMS/TAPES
Sufficient for classroom support.

BLAUSTEIN LIBRARY
American Jewish Committee
165 East 56th Street
New York, NY 10022
(212) 751-4000 Ext.297

177

GENERAL INFORMATION

HOURS OF SERVICE
9:30 a.m. to 5:30 p.m., Monday through Friday.

CONDITIONS OF ACCESS
Open only to qualified users, on appointment.

FACILITIES
Photocopier.

SIZE OF COLLECTIONS/HOLDINGS

GENERAL
35,000 books, 625 periodical titles, 20 vertical file drawers.

DESCRIPTION AND EVALUATION OF COLLECTION

LATIN AMERICAN HOLDINGS
Primarily consists of vertical file material concerning the past and present Jewish communities in each of the Latin American countries.

EVALUATION OF SUBJECT/AREA STRENGTH	Refer to page 110 for definitions of collection rating levels.

		Collection Rating Level (A-E)	
Subject Category		Monographs	Serials
1.	Bibliography & Reference	-	B
2.	Economics	-	-
3.	Education	-	-
4.	Geography & Anthropology	-	-
5.	History	-	-
6.	International Relations	-	-
7.	Language & Literature	-	-
8.	Law	-	-
9.	Military Affairs	-	-
10.	Philosophy & Religion	-	B-C
11.	Politics & Government	-	B-C
12.	Sociology	-	B-C

Area Category		Monographs	Serials
13.	Argentina	C	C
14.	Belize	B	B
15.	Bolivia	B	B
16.	Brazil	C	C
17.	Caribbean (excl. Cuba)	B	B
18.	Chile	B	B
19.	Colombia	B	B
20.	Costa Rica	B	B
21.	Cuba	B	B
22.	Dominican Republic	B	B
23.	Ecuador	B	B
24.	El Salvador	B	B
25.	Guatemala	B	B
26.	Guianas	B	B
27.	Haiti	B	B
28.	Honduras	B	B
29.	Jamaica	C	C
30.	Mexico	B	B
31.	Nicaragua	B	B
32.	Panama	B	B
33.	Paraguay	B	B
34.	Peru	B	B
35.	Uruguay	B	B
36.	Venezuela	B	B
37.	Other	B	B

SPECIAL COLLECTIONS

GOVERNMENT DOCUMENTS
Documents relevant to overall library interest.

MISCELLANEOUS VERTICAL FILES
Material on subjects and organizations predominantly concerned with the social sciences and specifically on the contemporary Jewish situation worldwide.

ARCHIVES AND MANUSCRIPTS
American Jewish Committee material for the period of 1906 - 1933. Material from 1934 to date is located in the Committee's Record Center Department.

ELMER HOLMES BOBST LIBRARY
New York University
70 Washington Square South
New York, NY 10012
(212) 998-2500

178

GENERAL INFORMATION

HOURS OF SERVICE
8:30 a.m. to 11:00 p.m., Monday through Thursday; 8:30 a.m. to 7:00 p.m., Friday; 10:00 a.m. to 6:00 p.m., Saturday; 2:00 p.m. to 10:00 p.m., Sunday.

CONDITIONS OF ACCESS
The following patron categories have access to the Bobst Library: Constituents (Students, Faculty and Staff of NYU); Research Libraries Group; Friends of Bobst Library; METRO; and Consortium member libraries (Cooper Union, New School and Parsons).

COOPERATIVE ARRANGEMENTS WITH OTHER INSTITUTIONS
The Library is a member of the following: RLG; METRO; and the Research Library Association of South Manhattan.

FACILITIES
Typewriters, microreader/printers, photocopiers, change machines.

SPECIAL SERVICES FOR THE HANDICAPPED
Special library assistance available for disabled NYU students only.

SIZE OF COLLECTIONS/HOLDINGS

GENERAL
Holdings: 2,000,000 volumes, 1,400,000 microform units and 16,000 serial titles. Special collections: Taminent Library (labor and radical materials); Robert F. Wagner Labor Archives; Fales Library of 19th and 20th Century American and English Literature; Berol Collection of Alice in Wonderland Materials; Rare Hebraica and Judaica; Remarque Collection; Robert Frost Collection; New York University Archives. Subject strengths: Business and Commerce, English Literature, Economics, UN Documents, English History, Latin American Area Studies and Middle Eastern Area Studies.

LATIN AMERICAN
Holdings: 36,000 volumes, 150 periodicals and 6 newspapers.

DESCRIPTION AND EVALUATION OF COLLECTIONS

LATIN AMERICAN HOLDINGS
The collection supports course work and research on many countries and a variety of subjects. Acquisitions have been highly selective and directed toward developing a representative collection of secondary sources on the history, politics, international relations, social and economic conditions, literatures and languages of Latin America and the Caribbean. Areas covered most consistently are the literature and political, economic and social history of Brazil, Mexico and Argentina. Resources on the Caribbean and Central America, and on Latin American art, music, business, cinema and popular culture, have improved in recent years.

EVALUATION OF
SUBJECT/AREA STRENGTH

Refer to page 110 for definitions of collection rating levels.

Subject Category		Collection Rating Level (A-E)	
		Monographs	Serials
1.	Bibliography & Reference	C	C
2.	Economics	B	B
3.	Education	A	A
4.	Geography & Anthropology	A-B	A-B
5.	History	B	B
6.	International Relations	A	A
7.	Language & Literature	C	C
8.	Law	A	A
9.	Military Affairs	A	A
10.	Philosophy & Religion	B	A
11.	Politics & Government	A	A
12.	Sociology	B	B

Area Category		Monographs	Serials
13.	Argentina	C	B
14.	Belize	A	A
15.	Bolivia	A	A
16.	Brazil	C	B
17.	Caribbean (excl. Cuba)	B	A
18.	Chile	A	A
19.	Colombia	A	A
20.	Costa Rica	B	A
21.	Cuba	B	A
22.	Dominican Republic	B	A
23.	Ecuador	A	A
24.	El Salvador	B	A
25.	Guatemala	B	A
26.	Guianas	A	A
27.	Haiti	B	A
28.	Honduras	B	A
29.	Jamaica	B	A
30.	Mexico	C	B
31.	Nicaragua	B	A
32.	Panama	B	A
33.	Paraguay	A	A
34.	Peru	B	A
35.	Uruguay	A	A
36.	Venezuela	A	A

SPECIAL COLLECTIONS

GOVERNMENT DOCUMENTS
The holdings of the Social Science/Documents Center include: statistical and congressional indexes; major statistical series; publications of international agencies such as the UN Economic Commission on Latin America, the Organization of the American States, the World Bank, the Intelligence Service Translations; and U.S. diplomatic history sources. Of particular importance are three microform sets: Latin America and Caribbean Official Statistical Serials by Chadwyck-Healey, covering 1890-1970s; the International Population Census Publications: Latin America and the Caribbean, covering 1945-1967; and the Annual Reports of the World's Central Banks by Chadwyck-Healey.

MISCELLANEOUS VERTICAL FILES
Working Papers (the Wilson Center, Kellog Institute, and Florida International University).

**CENTER FOR MIGRATION STUDIES (CMS)
LIBRARY AND ARCHIVES**
*209 Flagg Place
Staten Island, NY 10304
(718) 351-8800*

GENERAL INFORMATION

HOURS OF SERVICE
9:00 a.m. to 5:00 p.m., Monday through Friday.

CONDITIONS OF ACCESS
Unrestricted.

COOPERATIVE ARRANGEMENTS WITH OTHER INSTITUTIONS
CMS publications are exchanged with numerous research centers.

FACILITIES
Photocopier and microreader.

SIZE OF COLLECTIONS/HOLDINGS

GENERAL
20,000 titles; 250 serials; over 100 newsletters; 300 dissertations on microfilm; 40 newspapers; vertical file of journal articles; 33 processed archival collections.

LATIN AMERICAN
Approximately 550 titles; 11 serials; 10 newsletters; 15 dissertations; 2 newspapers; vertical file of clipped journal articles.

DESCRIPTION AND EVALUATION OF COLLECTION

LATIN AMERICAN HOLDINGS
The Latin American materials at CMS deal almost exclusively with topics relating to migration.

EVALUATION OF
SUBJECT/AREA STRENGTH

Refer to page 110 for definitions
of collection rating levels.

Subject Category		Collection Rating Level (A-E)	
		Monographs	Serials
1.	Bibliography & Reference	-	-
2.	Economics	-	-
3.	Education	-	-
4.	Geography & Anthropology	-	-
5.	History	-	-
6.	International Relations	B	-
7.	Language & Literature	-	-
8.	Law	-	-
9.	Military Affairs	-	-
10.	Philosophy & Religion	-	-
11.	Politics & Government	B	-
12.	Sociology	B	-

Area Category		Monographs	Serials
13.	Argentina	B	-
14.	Belize	-	-
15.	Bolivia	A	-
16.	Brazil	B	-
17.	Caribbean (excl. Cuba)	C	A
18.	Chile	B	-
19.	Colombia	A	-
20.	Costa Rica	-	-
21.	Cuba	B	-
22.	Dominican Republic	A	-
23.	Ecuador	-	-
24.	El Salvador	A	-
25.	Guatemala	B	-
26.	Guianas	-	-
27.	Haiti	B	A
28.	Honduras	A	-
29.	Jamaica	A	-
30.	Mexico	D	A
31.	Nicaragua	-	-
32.	Panama	A	-
33.	Paraguay	A	-
34.	Peru	B	-
35.	Uruguay	A	-
36.	Venezuela	B	-
37.	Other	C	A

SPECIAL COLLECTIONS

GOVERNMENT DOCUMENTS
Relatively few.

MISCELLANEOUS VERTICAL FILES
A small vertical file of clipped journal articles.

 MORRIS RAPHAEL COHEN LIBRARY
City College
of the City University of New York
North Academic Center
138th Street and Convent Avenue
New York, NY 10031
(212) 690-4292

GENERAL INFORMATION

HOURS OF SERVICE
9:00 a.m. to 8:00 p.m., Monday through Thursday; 9:00 a.m. to 5:00 p.m., Friday;
12:00 p.m. to 6:00 p.m., Saturday; 2:00 p.m. to 6:00 p.m., Sunday.

CONDITIONS OF ACCESS
Fairly unrestricted in-library use. Circulation restricted to CUNY students and faculty.

COOPERATIVE ARRANGEMENTS WITH OTHER INSTITUTIONS
CRL; METRO.

FACILITIES
Photocopiers; microfiche and microfilm reader/printers.

SPECIAL SERVICES FOR THE HANDICAPPED
Fully accessible to the handicapped.

SIZE OF COLLECTIONS/HOLDINGS

GENERAL
1,035,000 volumes, 525,000 book titles; 3,700 periodical subscriptions;
125,000 microforms; AV-total 13,215.

LATIN AMERICAN
The collection consists of about 10,000 titles on Latin America. Major periodicals dealing with Latin America are held.

DESCRIPTION AND EVALUATION OF COLLECTION

LATIN AMERICAN HOLDINGS
The Latin American holdings can support undergraduate and some graduate level work. The library is particularly strong in history and has built up the Caribbean and Puerto Rican Studies to support that department.

EVALUATION OF
SUBJECT/AREA STRENGTH

Refer to page 110 for definitions of collection rating levels.

Subject Category		Collection Rating Level (A-E)	
		Monographs	Serials
1.	Bibliography & Reference	C	C
2.	Economics	B	B
3.	Education	C	C
4.	Geography & Anthropology	B	B
5.	History	B	B
6.	International Relations	B	B
7.	Language & Literature	C	C
8.	Law	B	B
9.	Military Affairs	A	A
10.	Philosophy & Religion	B	B
11.	Politics & Government	B	B
12.	Sociology	B	B

Area Category		Monographs	Serials
13.	Argentina	A	A
14.	Belize	A	A
15.	Bolivia	A	A
16.	Brazil	A	A
17.	Caribbean (excl. Cuba)	B	B
18.	Chile	A	A
19.	Colombia	A	A
20.	Costa Rica	A	A
21.	Cuba	B	B
22.	Dominican Republic	B	B
23.	Ecuador	A	A
24.	El Salvador	A	A
25.	Guatemala	A	A

26.	Guianas	A	A
27.	Haiti	A	A
28.	Honduras	A	A
29.	Jamaica	A	A
30.	Mexico	A	A
31.	Nicaragua	A	A
32.	Panama	A	A
33.	Paraguay	A	A
34.	Peru	A	A
35.	Uruguay	A	A
36.	Venezuela	A	A
37.	Puerto Rico	B	B

SPECIAL COLLECTIONS

GOVERNMENT DOCUMENTS
Depository library since 1885. United Nations and OAS document collection.

MISCELLANEOUS VERTICAL FILES
Pamphlet files contain over 1,000 items dealing with Latin America. Pamphlets of the social sciences and education number 8,000.

ARCHIVES AND MANUSCRIPTS
Holdings are basically limited to materials about City College.

FILMS/TAPES
Film collection numbers 572. Videos consist of 120. A few on Latin America.

PROMINENT COLLECTIONS, RARE BOOKS, ETC.
Costume collection; British literature.

COLUMBIA UNIVERSITY LIBRARIES
535 West 114th Street
New York, NY 10027
(212) 280-3630

GENERAL INFORMATION

HOURS OF SERVICE
Same as general library hours. These vary depending on exams, intersession periods, holidays, and summer sessions.

CONDITIONS OF ACCESS
The collections are open to students, staff and faculty of Columbia University and affiliated institutions (Barnard College, Teachers College, and Union Theological Seminary). For special cases, consult the Library Information Office (280-2271).

COOPERATIVE ARRANGEMENTS WITH OTHER INSTITUTIONS
The Libraries have cooperative arrangements with RLG, METRO and LAMP .

FACILITIES
Photocopiers, microfilm equipment, microform readers and reader/printers.

SPECIAL SERVICES FOR THE HANDICAPPED
Accessible to the handicapped. Deputy borrower privilege cards may also be provided for members of the Columbia community. There is a Center for the Visually Handicapped at Lehman Library.

SIZE OF COLLECTIONS/HOLDINGS

GENERAL
5,551,719 volumes.

LATIN AMERICAN
Approximately 160,000 volumes and 1,500 periodical titles published in the area, of which about 600 are currently received.

DESCRIPTION AND EVALUATION OF COLLECTION

LATIN AMERICAN HOLDINGS
The collection is particularly strong in Argentina, Brazil, and Mexico. It emphasizes history, literature, law, politics, sociology and linguistics. Materials are mainly in Spanish and Portuguese.

EVALUATION OF SUBJECT/AREA STRENGTH	Refer to page 110 for definitions of collection rating levels.	
Subject Category	Collection Rating Level (A-E)	
	Monographs	Serials
1. Bibliography & Reference	D	D
2. Economics	C	C
3. Education	D	D*
4. Geography & Anthropology	C	C
5. History	D	C

* Includes Teachers College

6.	International Relations	D	D
7.	Language & Literature	D	D
8.	Law	D	D
9.	Military Affairs	C	C
10.	Philosophy & Religion	C	C
11.	Politics & Government	C	C
12.	Sociology	C	C

Area Category		Monographs	Serials
13.	Argentina	D	C
14.	Belize	B	A
15.	Bolivia	C	B
16.	Brazil	D	C
17.	Caribbean (excl. Cuba)	B	A
18.	Chile	C	B
19.	Colombia	C	B
20.	Costa Rica	C	B
21.	Cuba	C	B
22.	Dominican Republic	C	B
23.	Ecuador	C	B
24.	El Salvador	C	B
25.	Guatemala	C	B
26.	Guianas	B	A
27.	Haiti	B	A
28.	Honduras	C	B
29.	Jamaica	C	B
30.	Mexico	D	C
31.	Nicaragua	C	B
32.	Panama	D	C
33.	Paraguay	C	B
34.	Peru	D	C
35.	Uruguay	C	B
36.	Venezuela	C	B

SPECIAL COLLECTIONS

GOVERNMENT DOCUMENTS
Government documents are catalogued and housed in the various Columbia libraries according to subject. A collection of statistical yearbooks of all Latin American countries on microfiche is located in the Butler Library.

MISCELLANEOUS VERTICAL FILES
An extensive collection of vertical file materials in the social sciences, arranged by countries and subjects, is located in the Lehman Library.

ARCHIVES AND MANUSCRIPTS
The Frank Tannenbaum collection of correspondence, manuscripts and subject files from 1915 to 1969; The Carlos Diaz-Alejandro manuscripts and papers.

FILMS/TAPES
The Libraries do not acquire films or tapes on Latin America, but some may be acquired by university departments.

PROMINENT COLLECTIONS, RARE BOOKS, ETC.
The International Law Library has an outstanding collection of Latin American materials. Documents of the United Nations and OAS. The oral history collection on the labor movement in Argentina and Mexico.

COUNCIL ON FOREIGN RELATIONS LIBRARY
58 East 68th Street
New York, NY 10021
(212) 734-0400

GENERAL INFORMATION

HOURS OF SERVICE
9:00 a.m. to 5:00 p.m., Monday through Friday; closed on Fridays from June 15 through Labor Day.

CONDITIONS OF ACCESS
Introduction from member or instructor.

COOPERATIVE ARRANGEMENTS WITH OTHER INSTITUTIONS
Interlibrary loan.

FACILITIES
Photocopiers and microreaders.

SIZE OF COLLECTIONS/HOLDINGS

GENERAL
40,000 volumes; clipping files (12 newspapers clipped); U.S. Government Documents in subject area.

LATIN AMERICAN
1,000 volumes.

SPECIAL COLLECTIONS

GOVERNMENT DOCUMENTS
OAS, International Development Bank, UNCLA – some reports of each.

 DUANE LIBRARY
Fordham University
Bronx, NY 10458
(212) 579-2417

GENERAL INFORMATION

HOURS OF SERVICE
8:30 a.m. to 12:00 p.m., Monday through Thursday; 8:30 a.m. to 8:00 p.m., Friday; 9:00 a.m. to 6:00 p.m., Saturday; 12:00 noon to 12:00 a.m., Sunday.

CONDITIONS OF ACCESS
Reserved for Fordham students. METRO cards for others.

COOPERATIVE ARRANGEMENTS WITH OTHER INSTITUTIONS
METRO; New York Area Theological Libraries Association (NYATLA).

FACILITIES
Reproduction equipment, typewriters and microreaders.

SPECIAL SERVICES FOR THE HANDICAPPED
Kurtzweil reading machine.

SIZE OF COLLECTIONS/HOLDINGS

GENERAL
1.2 million volumes.

LATIN AMERICAN
Bibliography; 5,000 titles, including Puerto Rican and Latin American studies and Spanish-language literature.

DESCRIPTION AND EVALUATION OF COLLECTION

LATIN AMERICAN HOLDINGS
The Library maintains a collection of Latin American history for undergraduates.

SPECIAL COLLECTIONS

GOVERNMENT DOCUMENTS
Partial depository of government documents. Full collection of census material; UN records.

RAYMOND FOGELMAN LIBRARY
New School for Social Research
65 Fifth Avenue
New York, NY 10003
(212) 741-7906

GENERAL INFORMATION

HOURS OF SERVICE
10:00 a.m. to 10:30 p.m., Monday through Thursday; 10:00 a.m. to 6:00 p.m., Friday and Saturday.

CONDITIONS OF ACCESS
Open to New School students and others by special permission. METRO referrals accepted.

COOPERATIVE ARRANGEMENTS WITH OTHER INSTITUTIONS
The Library belongs to a library consortium together with New York University and Cooper Union.

FACILITIES
Microfilm readers and printers; coin-operated photocopiers; typewriters for student use only.

SIZE OF COLLECTIONS/HOLDINGS

GENERAL
As of June 1985, the Fogelman Library had approximately 138,000 titles in its collection and was receiving approximately 720 serial titles.

DESCRIPTION AND EVALUATION OF COLLECTION

LATIN AMERICAN HOLDINGS
Other than in the area of Cuba, the Latin American holdings at the Fogelman Library reflect the interest of New School researchers in specific topics, such as class formation, economic development and gender studies.

EVALUATION OF SUBJECT/AREA STRENGTH		Refer to page 110 for definitions of collection rating levels.

Subject Category		Collection Rating Level (A-E) Monographs
1.	Bibliography & Reference	B
2.	Economics	B
3.	Education	A
4.	Geography & Anthropology	A
5.	History	A
6.	International Relations	B
7.	Language & Literature	A
8.	Law	A
9.	Military Affairs	A
10.	Philosophy & Religion	A
11.	Politics & Government	B
12.	Sociology	B

Area Category		Monographs
13.	Argentina	A
14.	Belize	A
15.	Bolivia	A
16.	Brazil	A
17.	Caribbean (excl. Cuba)	A
18.	Chile	A
19.	Colombia	A
20.	Costa Rica	A
21.	Cuba	A
22.	Dominican Republic	A
23.	Ecuador	A
24.	El Salvador	A
25.	Guatemala	A
26.	Guianas	A
27.	Haiti	A
28.	Honduras	A
29.	Jamaica	A
30.	Mexico	A

31.	Nicaragua	A
32.	Panama	A
33.	Paraguay	A
34.	Peru	A
35.	Uruguay	A
36.	Venezuela	A
37.	Other	A

SPECIAL COLLECTIONS

GOVERNMENT DOCUMENTS
Minimal. The Library uses the Government Documents Collection and the International Documents Collection at New York University.

ARCHIVES AND MANUSCRIPTS
New School doctoral dissertations.

THE HISPANIC SOCIETY OF AMERICA LIBRARY
613 West 155th Street
New York, NY 10032
(212) 926-2234

185

GENERAL INFORMATION

HOURS OF SERVICE
1:00 p.m. to 4:30 p.m., Tuesday through Friday; 10:00 a.m. to 5:00 p.m., Saturday; closed Sunday.

CONDITIONS OF ACCESS
Open to the general public as well as specialists and researchers.

COOPERATIVE ARRANGEMENTS WITH OTHER INSTITUTIONS
An affiliate of the Hispanic Institute of the Library of Congress; no interlibrary loan.

SIZE OF COLLECTIONS/HOLDINGS

LATIN AMERICAN
About 80,000 items.

DESCRIPTION AND EVALUATION OF COLLECTION

LATIN AMERICAN HOLDINGS
Literature, criticism, history and culture to the end of the colonial period.

EVALUATION OF
SUBJECT/AREA STRENGTH

Refer to page 110 for definitions
of collection rating levels.

Subject Category		Collection Rating Level (A-E)	
		Monographs	Serials
1.	Bibliography & Reference	D	D
2.	Economics	-	-
3.	Education	-	-
4.	Geography & Anthropology	C	C
5.	History	D	D
6.	International Relations	C	C
7.	Language & Literature	D	D
8.	Law	B	B
9.	Military Affairs	A	-
10.	Philosophy & Religion	D	B
11.	Politics & Government	C	C
12.	Sociology	C	C

Area Category		Monographs	Serials
13.	Argentina	C	C
14.	Belize	C	C
15.	Bolivia	C	C
16.	Brazil	C	C
17.	Caribbean (excl. Cuba)	C	C
18.	Chile	C	C
19.	Colombia	C	C
20.	Costa Rica	C	C
21.	Cuba	C	C
22.	Dominican Republic	C	C
23.	Ecuador	C	C
24.	El Salvador	C	C
25.	Guatemala	C	C
26.	Guianas	C	C
27.	Haiti	C	C
28.	Honduras	C	C
29.	Jamaica	C	C
30.	Mexico	C	C
31.	Nicaragua	C	C

32.	Panama	C	C
33.	Paraguay	C	C
34.	Peru	C	C
35.	Uruguay	C	C
36.	Venezuela	C	C
37.	Other	C	C

SPECIAL COLLECTIONS

ARCHIVES AND MANUSCRIPTS
Strong collection.

FILMS/TAPES
Limited collection.

PROMINENT COLLECTIONS, RARE BOOKS, ETC.
Strong collection.

HUNTINGTON FREE LIBRARY
LIBRARY OF THE MUSEUM OF
THE AMERICAN INDIAN
9 Westchester Square
Bronx, NY 10461
(212) 829-7770

GENERAL INFORMATION

HOURS OF SERVICE
10:00 a.m. to 4:30 p.m., Monday through Friday; 10:00 a.m. to 4:30 p.m., first and third Saturdays of each month.

CONDITIONS OF ACCESS
Appointment and identification.

COOPERATIVE ARRANGEMENTS WITH OTHER INSTITUTIONS
METRO member.

FACILITIES
Microform reader/printer; photocopier.

SIZE OF COLLECTIONS/HOLDINGS

GENERAL
Approximately 40,000 books, journals, microforms and other materials.

LATIN AMERICAN
10,000.

DESCRIPTION AND EVALUATION OF COLLECTION

LATIN AMERICAN HOLDINGS
The Latin American holdings deal almost exclusively with the archæology, language and ethnology of the aboriginal population of the area. The Huntington Free Library is particularly strong in early imprints. It follows contemporary issues dealing with Indian populations. A good collection of dictionaries and grammars of Indian languages is held.

EVALUATION OF
SUBJECT/AREA STRENGTH

Refer to page 110 for definitions of collection rating levels.

Subject Category		Collection Rating Level (A-E)	
		Monographs	Serials
1.	Bibliography & Reference	C	C
2.	Economics	-	-
3.	Education	-	-
4.	Geography & Anthropology	C	C
5.	History	C	C
6.	International Relations	-	-
7.	Language & Literature	C	C
8.	Law	-	-
9.	Military Affairs	-	-
10.	Philosophy & Religion	-	-
11.	Politics & Government	-	-
12.	Sociology	-	-

SPECIAL COLLECTIONS

MISCELLANEOUS VERTICAL FILES
Subject files for the archæology of each country, as well as individual Indian groups; considerable old, hard-to-locate material.

ARCHIVES AND MANUSCRIPTS
Philip I. Valentini's notes on Maya sites (Palenque and others); Rodolfo Schuller's papers on Central American tribes and linguistics.

PROMINENT COLLECTIONS, RARE BOOKS, ETC.
Excellent collection of rare books dealing with early contacts, codices, etc. (e.g. Gomara, Herrera, Kingsborough, Humboldt).

ICARUS FILMS 187
200 Park Avenue South, No.1319
New York, NY 10003
(212) 674-3375

GENERAL INFORMATION

HOURS OF SERVICE
9:30 a.m. to 5:30 p.m., Monday through Friday.

CONDITIONS OF ACCESS
Films and home video-cassettes can be purchased; they can also be rented, or previewed for purchase consideration.

FACILITIES
Latin American Film Library.

SIZE OF COLLECTIONS/HOLDINGS

GENERAL
124 films.

LATIN AMERICAN
48 films and videos.

DESCRIPTION AND EVALUATION OF COLLECTION

LATIN AMERICAN HOLDINGS
The Latin American Film Library contains 48 films and videotapes chosen to communicate the evolving reality of Latin America to North American audiences. It has the largest and most comprehensive collection of films and videotapes on Central America available in this country.

EVALUATION OF SUBJECT/AREA STRENGTH

Refer to page 110 for definitions of collection rating levels.

Area Category		Collection Rating Level (A-E) Films
13.	Argentina	A
14.	Belize	-
15.	Bolivia	-
16.	Brazil	B
17.	Caribbean (excl. Cuba)	-
18.	Chile	B
19.	Colombia	A
20.	Costa Rica	-
21.	Cuba	A
22.	Dominican Republic	C
23.	Ecuador	-
24.	El Salvador	B
25.	Guatemala	C
26.	Guianas	-
27.	Haiti	A
28.	Honduras	A
29.	Jamaica	-
30.	Mexico	-
31.	Nicaragua	E
32.	Panama	-
33.	Paraguay	-
34.	Peru	B
35.	Puerto Rico	A
36.	Uruguay	B
37.	Venezuela	-

PAUL KLAPPER LIBRARY
Queens College of the
City University of New York
Kissena Boulevard
Flushing, NY 11367
(718) 520-2842

GENERAL INFORMATION

HOURS OF SERVICE
9:00 a.m. to 9:00 p.m., Monday through Thursday; 9:00 a.m. to 5:00 p.m., Friday; 12:00 a.m. to 5:00 p.m., Saturday and Sunday.

CONDITIONS OF ACCESS
CUNY students have all privileges. Alumni and general public have restricted access.

COOPERATIVE ARRANGEMENTS WITH OTHER INSTITUTIONS
CUNY students enjoy borrowing privileges.

FACILITIES
Photocopiers, microreaders.

SIZE OF COLLECTIONS/HOLDINGS

GENERAL
More than 500,000 titles.

LATIN AMERICAN
5,000 titles.

DESCRIPTION AND EVALUATION OF COLLECTION

LATIN AMERICAN HOLDINGS
The Latin American collection covers all countries and subjects related to Latin America and the Caribbean area. The greatest collecting effort is directed toward materials on contemporary Latin America, although strong on colonial Brazil. Emphasis is on Brazil, Colombia, Ecuador, Peru and the Caribbean area, including Cuba. It concentrates primarily on the history, literature, political science and economics of those countries.

EVALUATION OF SUBJECT/AREA STRENGTH	Refer to page 110 for definitions of collection rating levels.	
	Collection Rating Level (A-E)	
Subject Category	Monographs	Serials
1. Bibliography & Reference	C	B
2. Economics	C	A
3. Education	A	A
4. Geography & Anthropology	C	A
5. History	C	A
6. International Relations	C	A
7. Language & Literature	C	B
8. Law	A	A
9. Military Affairs	A	A
10. Philosophy & Religion	A	A
11. Politics & Government	C	A
12. Sociology	C	A

Area Category		Monographs	Serials
13.	Argentina	B	A
14.	Belize	-	-
15.	Bolivia	A	A
16.	Brazil	D	B
17.	Caribbean (excl. Cuba)	C	B
18.	Chile	B	A
19.	Colombia	C	B
20.	Costa Rica	B	A
21.	Cuba	C	A
22.	Dominican Republic	C	A
23.	Ecuador	B	A
24.	El Salvador	B	A
25.	Guatemala	B	A
26.	Guianas	A	A
27.	Haiti	B	A
28.	Honduras	A	A
29.	Jamaica	A	A
30.	Mexico	C	A
31.	Nicaragua	C	A
32.	Panama	A	A
33.	Paraguay	A	A
34.	Peru	C	A
35.	Uruguay	B	A
36.	Venezuela	B	A
37.	Other	-	-

SPECIAL COLLECTIONS

PROMINENT COLLECTIONS, RARE BOOKS, ETC.
Brasiliana; Coleção Documentos Brasileiros.

HERBERT H. LEHMAN LIBRARY
Herbert H. Lehman College
of the City University of New York
Bedford Park Boulevard West
Bronx, NY 10468
(212) 960-8577

189

GENERAL INFORMATION

HOURS OF SERVICE
8:30 a.m. to 10:30 p.m., Monday through Thursday; 8:30 a.m. to 4:30 p.m., Friday; 10:00 a.m. to 5:00 p.m., Saturday; 12:00 a.m. to 7:00 p.m., Sunday.

CONDITIONS OF ACCESS
CUNY ID; other colleges: METRO card; all others: current ID card (driver's license, s.s. card) to obtain one day pass at the reference desk.

FACILITIES
Photocopiers, microfilm reader/printers, microfiche readers are available.

SPECIAL SERVICES FOR THE HANDICAPPED
Telephone answering machine for the deaf.

SIZE OF COLLECTIONS/HOLDINGS

GENERAL
An estimated 500,000 volumes.

DESCRIPTION AND EVALUATION OF COLLECTION

LATIN AMERICAN HOLDINGS
The Lehman Latin American collection includes all major reference works. Special emphasis is given to Puerto Rican Studies concentrating on history and literature. History, literature and political science are widely collected for all Latin America with emphasis on contemporary literary works. Periodical holdings are limited with most published in the U. S.

EVALUATION OF   Refer to page 110 for definitions
SUBJECT/AREA STRENGTH   of collection rating levels.

Subject Category	Collection Rating Level (A-E) Monographs
1. Bibliography & Reference	A
2. Economics	A
3. Education	A
4. Geography & Anthropology	A
5. History	B
6. International Relations	A
7. Language & Literature	B
8. Law	-
9. Military Affairs	-
10. Philosophy & Religion	-
11. Politics & Government	A
12. Sociology	A

Area Category	Monographs
13. Argentina	A
14. Belize	-
15. Bolivia	A
16. Brazil	A
17. Caribbean (excl. Cuba)	A
18. Chile	A
19. Colombia	A
20. Costa Rica	A
21. Cuba	A
22. Dominican Republic	A
23. Ecuador	A
24. El Salvador	A
25. Guatemala	A
26. Guianas	-
27. Haiti	A
28. Honduras	A
29. Jamaica	A
30. Mexico	A
31. Nicaragua	A
32. Panama	A
33. Paraguay	A
34. Peru	A
35. Uruguay	A
36. Venezuela	A
37. Other	-

SPECIAL COLLECTIONS

GOVERNMENT DOCUMENTS
Selective.

ARCHIVES AND MANUSCRIPTS
Bronx materials.

FILMS/TAPES
Limited.

PROMINENT COLLECTIONS, RARE BOOKS, ETC.
Oral histories of the Bronx.

LIBRARY FOR CARIBBEAN RESEARCH
Research Institute for the Study of Man
162 East 78th Street
New York, NY 10021
(212) 535-8448

GENERAL INFORMATION

HOURS OF SERVICE
9:00 a.m. to 5:00 p.m., Monday through Friday.

FACILITIES
Photocopier.

SIZE OF COLLECTIONS/HOLDINGS

GENERAL
Total: 15,000 volumes, 180 periodicals.

LATIN AMERICAN
Caribbean (primarily non-Hispanic): 12,000 volumes.

DESCRIPTION AND EVALUATION OF COLLECTIONS

CARIBBEAN HOLDINGS
The Library has a comprehensive collection of books, dissertations and journals on the non- Hispanic Caribbean. There are also collections of reprints, pamphlets, and other vertical file holdings. All aspects of life in the region are covered, with

emphasis on the social sciences and culture. Government documents are collected from both the U.S. and the Caribbean. The library maintains, as an integral part of the card catalog, a periodical index (by author and subject) of articles on the non-Hispanic Caribbean from journals received.

EVALUATION OF SUBJECT/AREA STRENGTH		Refer to page 110 for definitions of collection rating levels.*

Subject Category		Collection Rating Level (A-E)	
		Monographs	Serials
1.	Bibliography & Reference	D	D
2.	Economics	E	C
3.	Education	C	C
4.	Geography & Anthropology	E	E
5.	History	E	E
6.	International Relations	D	D
7.	Language & Literature	C	C
8.	Law	C	C
9.	Military Affairs	B	B
10.	Philosophy & Religion	E	E
11.	Politics & Government	E	E
12.	Sociology	E	E

Area Category		Monographs	Serials
13.	Belize	C	C
14.	Caribbean (excl. Cuba)	E	D
15.	Dominican Republic	D	C
16.	Guianas	E	D
17.	Haiti	E	D
18.	Jamaica	E	E
19.	Trinidad & Barbados	D	D

* The aim of the Library is to achieve category E in all levels of research which relate to the non-Hispanic Caribbean.

SPECIAL COLLECTIONS

GOVERNMENT DOCUMENTS
U.S., Caribbean and British government documents are integrated into the collection as a whole. The Library receives many statistical publications from the Caribbean region and many documents from the U.S. government as well.

MISCELLANEOUS VERTICAL FILES
There are 12 vertical file drawers at present, and the collection is growing.

McLAUGHLIN LIBRARY
Seton Hall University

400 South Orange Avenue
South Orange, NJ 07079
(201) 761-9431

GENERAL INFORMATION

HOURS OF SERVICE
8:00 a.m. to 11:00 p.m., Monday through Thursday; 8:00 a.m. to 5:00 p.m., Friday; 9:00 a.m. to 5:00 p.m., Saturday; 1:00 p.m. to 11:00 p.m., Sunday.

CONDITIONS OF ACCESS
SHU Library card or CECLS card or Special Borrower's card.

COOPERATIVE ARRANGEMENTS WITH OTHER INSTITUTIONS
CECLS (County of Essex Cooperative System).

FACILITIES
Photocopiers, microform readers and reader/printers; literature search services by computer, Infotrac, IBM PC's.

SPECIAL SERVICES FOR THE HANDICAPPED
Ramps, elevator and personal assistance as needed.

SIZE OF COLLECTIONS/HOLDINGS

GENERAL
Approximately 335,000.

LATIN AMERICAN
The collection consists of approximately 4,500 books.

DESCRIPTION AND EVALUATION OF COLLECTION

LATIN AMERICAN HOLDINGS
The Latin American collection is up-to-date and appropriate for curricular related materials. The holdings include bibliographic guides, reference materials, anthologies and literature in translation.

EVALUATION OF
SUBJECT/AREA STRENGTH

Refer to page 110 for definitions
of collection rating levels.

Subject Category		Collection Rating Level (A-E)	
		Monographs	Serials
1.	Bibliography & Reference	D	D
2.	Economics	D	D
3.	Education	D	D
4.	Geography & Anthropology	B	B
5.	History	D	D
6.	International Relations	D	D
7.	Language & Literature	B	B
8.	Law	B	B
9.	Military Affairs	B	B
10.	Philosophy & Religion	D	D
11.	Politics & Government	D	D
12.	Sociology	D	D

Area Category		Monographs	Serials
13.	Argentina	A	A
14.	Belize	A	A
15.	Bolivia	A	A
16.	Brazil	A	A
17.	Caribbean (excl. Cuba)	A	A
18.	Chile	A	A
19.	Colombia	A	A
20.	Costa Rica	A	A
21.	Cuba	B	B
22.	Dominican Republic	A	A
23.	Ecuador	A	A
24.	El Salvador	A	A
25.	Guatemala	A	A
26.	Guianas	A	A
27.	Haiti	A	A
28.	Honduras	A	A
29.	Jamaica	A	A
30.	Mexico	B	B
31.	Nicaragua	A	A
32.	Panama	A	A
33.	Paraguay	A	A
34.	Peru	A	A
35.	Uruguay	A	A
36.	Venezuela	A	A
37.	Other	A	A

SPECIAL COLLECTIONS

GOVERNMENT DOCUMENTS
New Jersey State Documents; selected U.S. Government Depository.

MISCELLANEOUS VERTICAL FILES
General Collection; New Jersey materials; maps.

ARCHIVES AND MANUSCRIPTS
Archdiocese of Newark Archives and Seton Hall University Archives, by appointment (761-7052).

FILMS/TAPES
Educational Media Center(761-9429).

PROMINENT COLLECTIONS, RARE BOOKS, ETC.
Rare Book Room; Archdiocese of Newark Seminary Library (761-9198).

NATIONAL BROADCASTING CORPORATION (NBC)
Reference Library
30 Rockefeller Plaza
New York, NY 10112
(212) 664-5307

192

GENERAL INFORMATION

HOURS OF SERVICE
9:00 a.m. to 7:30 p.m., Monday through Friday.

CONDITIONS OF ACCESS
NBC employees; limited access to other professionals, by appointment only. Fee-based services are available to outside users.

COOPERATIVE ARRANGEMENTS WITH OTHER INSTITUTIONS
Informal cooperative arrangements with numerous other corporate libraries.

FACILITIES
Two photocopiers, three microphoto copiers; various computer terminals and PCs; Rapicom Fax machine.

SIZE OF COLLECTIONS/HOLDINGS

GENERAL
Approximately 15,000 books, 200 periodical subscriptions, 80 vertical file drawers, 7,000 microfilm reels. Subscribes to fourteen database systems, including NEXIS and Dialog. Broad subject coverage, with emphasis on current affairs, arts/ entertainment, business, biography and history.

LATIN AMERICAN
Books on Latin America number approximately 100, including both general titles and country-specific titles. Numerous other reference books contain extensive material on Latin America. The Library does not subscribe to any specialized Latin America periodicals, but does subscribe to a number of current affairs journals that include material on Latin America. There are also clip files on Latin America and individual countries. In addition, the Library has access to Latin American newsletters on NEXIS.

 NEW YORK BOTANICAL GARDEN LIBRARY
Southern Boulevard
Bronx, NY 10458
(212) 220-8753

GENERAL INFORMATION

HOURS OF SERVICE
Academic year: 9:30 a.m. to 6:00 p.m., Monday through Thursday; 9:30 a.m. to 4:00 p.m., Friday and Saturday. Summer: 9:30 a.m. to 4:00 p.m., Monday through Friday.

CONDITIONS OF ACCESS
Collections available to anyone seeking information or wishing to use materials on site. Books and monographs are lent on interlibrary loan; journals can be photocopied.

COOPERATIVE ARRANGEMENTS WITH OTHER INSTITUTIONS
Member of METRO, OCLC.

FACILITIES
Database searches, photocopying available on site for a fee.

SIZE OF COLLECTIONS/HOLDINGS

GENERAL
The Garden Library's research collections include 184,000 volumes, 8,900 serial titles, 44,000 microforms, 102,000 reprints and pamphlets, 425,000 manuscripts and archives, 100,000 photographs and slides, 10,000 items of botanical art, 14,000 architectural drawings and 3,600 artifacts.

DESCRIPTION AND EVALUATION OF COLLECTION

LATIN AMERICAN HOLDINGS
Latin American and Caribbean holdings include books, journals, blueprints and maps on botany, horticulture and related fields such as ecology, geology, paleobotany and agriculture. Latin American materials are actively acquired.

EVALUATION OF
SUBJECT/AREA STRENGTH

Refer to page 110 for definitions of collection rating levels.

Subject Category		Collection Rating Level (A-E)	
		Monographs	Serials
1.	Bibliography & Reference	A-E	-
2.	Economics	-	-
3.	Education	-	-
4.	Geography & Anthropology	A-E	-
5.	History	-	-
6.	International Relations	-	-
7.	Language & Literature	-	-
8.	Law	-	-
9.	Military Affairs	-	-
10.	Philosophy & Religion	-	-
11.	Politics & Government	-	-
12.	Sociology	-	-

Area Category		Monographs	Serials
13.	Argentina	B-E	-
14.	Belize	B-E	-
15.	Bolivia	B-E	-
16.	Brazil	B-E	-
17.	Caribbean (excl. Cuba)	B-E	-
18.	Chile	B-E	-
19.	Colombia	B-E	-
20.	Costa Rica	B-E	-
21.	Cuba	B-E	-

22.	Dominican Republic	B-E	-
23.	Ecuador	B-E	-
24.	El Salvador	B-E	-
25.	Guatemala	B-E	-
26.	Guianas	B-E	-
27.	Haiti	B-E	-
28.	Honduras	B-E	-
29.	Jamaica	B-E	-
30.	Mexico	B-E	-
31.	Nicaragua	B-E	-
32.	Panama	B-E	-
33.	Paraguay	B-E	-
34.	Peru	B-E	-
35.	Uruguay	B-E	-
36.	Venezuela	B-E	-
37.	Other	B-E	-

 NEW YORK PUBLIC LIBRARY (NYPL)
ASTOR, LENOX AND TILDEN FOUNDATION
Research Libraries
42nd Street and 5th Avenue
New York, NY 10018
(212) 930-0800

GENERAL INFORMATION

HOURS OF SERVICE
Hours of service vary since schedules of departments within the Research
Libraries differ from one another.

CONDITIONS OF ACCESS
Material is available to all but for reference only. Cards of admission to Special Collections (e.g. Rare Books, Mss. & Archives) must be applied for at Office of Special Collections.

COOPERATIVE ARRANGEMENTS WITH OTHER INSTITUTIONS
Material not available on interlibrary loan except with members of RLG and then
only as a library of last resort. Photocopies are available free through cooperative
arrangements through RLG or NYSILL, or by fee from the Library's Photographic
Services.

FACILITIES
Microreaders as well as facilities for reproducing materials are available.

SIZE OF COLLECTIONS/HOLDINGS

GENERAL
At present, the Research Libraries' collections number some 6 million books or book-like materials. The majority of the collections have true breadth and depth. Strengths are in the arts, humanities, social sciences and the physical sciences.

LATIN AMERICAN
It is extremely difficult to assess the size of the Latin American and Caribbean collections since they are scattered throughout the Research Libraries. The best estimate would be in the area of 150,000- 200,000 volumes.

DESCRIPTION AND EVALUATION OF COLLECTION

LATIN AMERICAN HOLDINGS
NYPL began collecting early in this field. There are strengths as well as treasures in the original Astor and Lenox NYPL collections. The library continues to build on these strengths. Emphasis has been on the arts, humanities and social sciences. The great strengths are in the material on early voyages and discoveries, as well as anthropology, history, language and literature. Geographically speaking, the Mexican and Haitian collections are probably the strongest. The library does not collect medicine, pedagogy or theology (but it does collect extensively in philosophy and history of religious movements) and only selectively in law (history and philosophy of law, public and international law) and the life sciences. NYPL collects periodicals extensively and newspapers only selectively.

EVALUATION OF SUBJECT/AREA STRENGTH		Refer to page 110 for definitions of collection rating levels.	
		Collection Rating Level (A-E)	
Subject Category		Monographs	Serials
1.	Bibliography & Reference	D	D
2.	Economics	D	D
3.	Education	B	B
4.	Geography & Anthropology	D	D
5.	History	D	D
6.	International Relations	D	D
7.	Language & Literature	D	D
8.	Law	B	B
9.	Military Affairs	D	D
10.	Philosophy & Religion	C	C
11.	Politics & Government	D	D
12.	Sociology	D	D

Area Category		Monographs	Serials
13.	Argentina	D	D
14.	Belize	D	D
15.	Bolivia	D	D
16.	Brazil	D	D
17.	Caribbean (excl. Cuba)	D	D
18.	Chile	D	D
19.	Colombia	D	D
20.	Costa Rica	D	D
21.	Cuba	D	D
22.	Dominican Republic	D	D
23.	Ecuador	D	D
24.	El Salvador	D	D
25.	Guatemala	D	D
26.	Guianas	D	D
27.	Haiti	D	D
28.	Honduras	D	D
29.	Jamaica	D	D
30.	Mexico	D	D
31.	Nicaragua	D	D
32.	Panama	C	C
33.	Paraguay	D	D
34.	Peru	D	D
35.	Uruguay	D	D
36.	Venezuela	D	D
37.	Other	D	D

SPECIAL COLLECTIONS

GOVERNMENT DOCUMENTS
A strong collection, particularly for the 20th century. National gazettes from the earlier periods to the present. Particular areas of interest for the library have always been statistical publications, demography, banking and foreign trade.

ARCHIVES AND MANUSCRIPTS
A notable repository is the Obadiah Rich collection which contains both original documents and transcripts of archives concerning the administration of Spanish colonies in America.

FILMS/TAPES
There is an excellent collection of audio-visual material on Caribbean music and culture at the Schomburg Center for Research in Black Culture.

PROMINENT COLLECTIONS, RARE BOOKS, ETC.
A rich collection of early materials notably in the area of voyages and discovery of the New World as well as early Mexican imprints. There is a strong collection of 19th and 20th century photographs of the Caribbean at the Schomburg Center.

THE NEW YORK CITY PUBLIC LIBRARY
The Schomburg Center
for Research in Black Culture
515 Lenox Avenue
New York, NY 10037
(212) 862-4000

GENERAL INFORMATION

HOURS OF SERVICE
12:00 p.m. to 8:00 p.m., Monday through Wednesday; 10:00 a.m. to 6:00 p.m., Thursday through Saturday (summer hours vary).

CONDITIONS OF ACCESS
Researchers must be 18 years old and over; present legible identification with name and address; special collections require registration.

COOPERATIVE ARRANGEMENTS WITH OTHER INSTITUTIONS
Participates in METRO, RLG, NYSILL.

FACILITIES
Photocopiers, microfilm machines; reproduction facilities available for photographs.

SPECIAL SERVICES FOR THE HANDICAPPED
No special services provided beyond accessibility to building and elevators.

SIZE OF COLLECTIONS/HOLDINGS

GENERAL
Schomburg Center's aim is to document the history and culture of peoples of African descent throughout the world. General collection is very strong on Afro-American population of the U.S., African people on the continent and Black population of Western Hemisphere. Of the approximately 97,000 volumes in the general collection, an estimated 15-20% deal with Afro-Hispanic and Afro-Caribbean history and culture. Coverage of Latin America is more intense for those countries with sizeable Black populations such as Brazil, Guyana, Venezuela, Colombia.

But library also has books on the Black experience as far afield as Uruguay and Argentina. All of the Caribbean countries are within collecting scope. Publications are in most of the regional languages including English, French, Spanish, Portuguese, some Dutch, Danish and various creole languages. Of the 709 current periodicals and newspapers, 8 are from South America and 77 are published in the Caribbean.

DESCRIPTION AND EVALUATION OF COLLECTION

LATIN AMERICAN HOLDINGS
As the level of scholarship in the library's collecting area improves and the reliability of its local dealers and contacts improve, so do its holdings increase in depth and breadth. All of the above factors have combined to make the Schomburg Center's collections on Black people in the Americas capable of supporting advanced research. In addition to the book and periodical holdings, Schomburg has extensive manuscript, photograph, vertical file, record, tape and film holdings.

EVALUATION OF SUBJECT/AREA STRENGTH		Refer to page 110 for definitions of collection rating levels.	
		Collection Rating Level (A-E)	
Subject Category		Monographs	Serials
1.	Bibliography & Reference	C	C
2.	Economics	A	C
3.	Education	C	C
4.	Geography & Anthropology	C	C
5.	History	D	D
6.	International Relations	C	D
7.	Language & Literature	E	D
8.	Law	A	A
9.	Military Affairs	A	-
10.	Philosophy & Religion	D	D
11.	Politics & Government	E	D
12.	Sociology	C	C

Area Category		Monographs	Serials
13.	Argentina	B	-
14.	Belize	C	A
15.	Bolivia	A	-
16.	Brazil	E	B
17.	Caribbean (excl. Cuba)	E	D
18.	Chile	A	-

19.	Colombia	D	-
20.	Costa Rica	A	-
21.	Cuba	E	C
22.	Dominican Republic	B	-
23.	Ecuador	A	-
24.	El Salvador	A	-
25.	Guatemala	A	-
26.	Guianas	E	A
27.	Haiti	E	D
28.	Honduras	A	-
29.	Jamaica	E	C
30.	Mexico	A	A
31.	Nicaragua	A	-
32.	Panama	D	A
33.	Paraguay	A	-
34.	Peru	A	-
35.	Uruguay	A	-
36.	Venezuela	C	A
37.	Suriname	D	A

SPECIAL COLLECTIONS

GOVERNMENT DOCUMENTS
These are collected by the Economics and Public Affairs Division, N.Y.P.L., 42nd Street and Fifth Avenue. The Schomburg Center acquires documents on a very selective basis.

MISCELLANEOUS VERTICAL FILES
The vertical files contain over 7,000 subject headings, many of which relate to the Carribean and South America. Material selected for VF include news clips, broadsides, fliers and invitations. Older VF on microfiche document both prominent and obscure Afro-Hispanic and Caribbean individuals, organizations and institutions.

ARCHIVES AND MANUSCRIPTS
Archives contain a broad range of material relating to the Caribbean and individuals of Caribbean origin. For example, holdings include papers of pœt Nicolas Guillen, novelist and pœt Claude McKay, entertainer Eusebia Cosme (from Cuba) and U.N.I.A. leader Marcus Garvey. Haitian manuscript holdings are the strongest, but other collections document the slavery experience in Jamaica, Puerto Rico, Martinique and Guadeloupe.

FILMS/TAPES
Moving Image and Recorded Sound (MIRS) Section contains film and videotapes on Black history and culture of Caribbean; oral history tapes on prominent Caribbean-Americans and recorded speeches. Musical recordings include the African-based music of the Caribbean and South America.

PROMINENT COLLECTIONS, RARE BOOKS, ETC.
Rare books collection numbers over one thousand items. The oldest book on South America dates from 1627, but many others published in the eighteenth and nineteenth centuries cover themes of discovery and exploration; literary works; history and religion. The Kaiser Index to Black Resources is a unique bibliographic finding aid which indexes Black periodicals and newspapers as well as other sources of information from 1945 to the present. It contains citations about Caribbean individuals and organizations and other miscellaneous references.

PHOTOGRAPHS
Total collection numbers over 200,000 items, of which approximately 10% deal with the Caribbean and South America. Most of these date from the twentieth century, but Schomburg has over 5,000 photographs from the nineteenth century representing the variety of reprographic techniques available, such as calotype, ambrotype, albumen prints and daguerrotype. Countries represented in holdings include Brazil, Cuba, Peru, Chile, Colombia and Panama.

**NEW YORK UNIVERSITY
GRADUATE SCHOOL OF
BUSINESS ADMINISTRATION LIBRARY**
19 Rector Street, 2nd Floor
New York, NY 10006
(212) 285-6231

GENERAL INFORMATION

HOURS OF SERVICE
9:00 a.m. to 10:00 p.m., Monday through Thursday; 9:00 a.m. to 6:00 p.m., Friday; 10:00 a.m. to 6:00 p.m., Saturday.

CONDITIONS OF ACCESS
NYU students, faculty and staff. Other users by special arrangement.

COOPERATIVE ARRANGEMENTS WITH OTHER INSTITUTIONS
RLG, METRO.

FACILITIES
5 photocopiers; 6 microform reader/printers.

SIZE OF COLLECTIONS/HOLDINGS

GENERAL
105,000 volumes.

DESCRIPTION AND EVALUATION OF COLLECTION

LATIN AMERICAN HOLDINGS
The Library maintains a standard collection of volumes on marketing, management and statistical information.

EVALUATION OF   Refer to page 110 for definitions
SUBJECT/AREA STRENGTH   of collection rating levels.

Subject Category		Collection Rating Level (A-E)	
		Monographs	Serials
1.	Bibliography & Reference	A	A
2.	Economics	A	A
3.	Education	-	-
4.	Geography & Anthropology	-	-
5.	History	-	-
6.	International Relations	-	-
7.	Language & Literature	-	-
8.	Law	-	-
9.	Military Affairs	-	-
10.	Philosophy & Religion	-	-
11.	Politics & Government	-	-
12.	Sociology	-	-

**NEW YORK UNIVERSITY
SCHOOL OF LAW LIBRARY**   197
*40 Washington Square South
New York, NY 10012
(212) 998-6300*

GENERAL INFORMATION

HOURS OF SERVICE
8:00 a.m. to 11:30 p.m., Monday through Friday; 9:00 a.m. to 11:30 p.m., Saturday; 12:00 p.m. to 11:30 p.m., Sunday.

CONDITIONS OF ACCESS
NYU students and faculty. Outside users by arrangement.

COOPERATIVE ARRANGEMENTS WITH OTHER INSTITUTIONS
METRO; reciprocity with Columbia Law Library.

FACILITIES
Microform: 16 reader-printers; audio-visual: 12 reader-printers; 25 computers
(NYU students only); 10 photocopiers.

SIZE OF COLLECTIONS/HOLDINGS

GENERAL
730,000 volumes/volume equivalents.

DESCRIPTION AND EVALUATION OF COLLECTION

LATIN AMERICAN HOLDINGS
Primary sources from all countries; statutes and decisions. A noncomprehensive
collection of periodicals, serials, treatises with special emphasis on Argentina,
Brazil and Chile.

EVALUATION OF SUBJECT/AREA STRENGTH		Refer to page 110 for definitions of collection rating levels.	
		Collection Rating Level (A-E)	
Subject Category		Monographs	Serials
1.	Bibliography & Reference	-	-
2.	Economics	-	-
3.	Education	-	-
4.	Geography & Anthropology	-	-
5.	History	-	-
6.	International Relations	-	-
7.	Language & Literature	-	-
8.	Law	B	B
9.	Military Affairs	-	-
10.	Philosophy & Religion	-	-
11.	Politics & Government	-	-
12.	Sociology	-	-

Area Category		Monographs	Serials
13.	Argentina	C	C
14.	Belize	B	B
15.	Bolivia	B	B
16.	Brazil	C	C
17.	Caribbean (excl. Cuba)	B	B
18.	Chile	C	C
19.	Colombia	B	B
20.	Costa Rica	B	B
21.	Cuba	B	B
22.	Dominican Republic	B	B
23.	Ecuador	C	C
24.	El Salvador	C	C
25.	Guatemala	B	B
26.	Guianas	B	B
27.	Haiti	B	B
28.	Honduras	B	B
29.	Jamaica	B	B
30.	Mexico	C	C
31.	Nicaragua	B	B
32.	Panama	B	B
33.	Paraguay	B	B
34.	Peru	B	B
35.	Uruguay	B	B
36.	Venezuela	B	B
37.	Other	B	B

SPECIAL COLLECTIONS

GOVERNMENT DOCUMENTS
Collection of OAS documents.

PACE UNIVERSITY LIBRARY
Pace Plaza
New York, NY 10038
(212) 488-1667

198

GENERAL INFORMATION

HOURS OF SERVICE
Call for information.

CONDITIONS OF ACCESS
METRO card or prior arrangement.

COOPERATIVE ARRANGEMENTS WITH OTHER INSTITUTIONS
METRO.

FACILITIES
The library maintains the standard equipment expected in an academic library.

SIZE OF COLLECTIONS/HOLDINGS

GENERAL
340,000 volumes, 1,500 periodical subscriptions.

LATIN AMERICAN
Several thousand.

DESCRIPTION AND EVALUATION OF COLLECTION

LATIN AMERICAN HOLDINGS
Pace has a good Latin America and Caribbean collection (level "B" for the most part), in response to curriculum needs, and to support the presumed cultural interests of the considerable number of Latin American and Caribbean students on the NYC campus. However, the library does not subscribe to periodicals published in Latin America (with the exception of Central Bank journals), nor does it have much that is not in the English language. Pace catalogs its holdings per OCLC; retrospective conversion has proceeded to include almost all materials that could be considered pertinent to Latin American and Caribbean studies.

SPECIAL COLLECTIONS

GOVERNMENT DOCUMENTS
Selected; only U.S. and international; some Central Bank materials.

MISCELLANEOUS VERTICAL FILES
Annual corporate reports of Latin American companies (selected).

MINA REES LIBRARY
The Graduate School & University Center
City University of New York
33 West 42nd Street
New York, NY 10036
(212) 642-2874

199

GENERAL INFORMATION

HOURS OF SERVICE
Academic year: 9:00 a.m. to 9:00 p.m., Monday through Thursday; 9:00 a.m. to 5:00 p.m., Friday; closed to the public on Saturday. Summer hours: 9:00 a.m. to 5:00 p.m., Monday through Friday.

CONDITIONS OF ACCESS
Open to non-CUNY who have need of this collection, upon presentation of appropriate identification (photo-ID, driver's license, etc.).

COOPERATIVE ARRANGEMENTS WITH OTHER INSTITUTIONS
Member of METRO, OCLC and CRL.

FACILITIES
Coin operated, self-service photocopiers, microfilm and microfiche readers and reader-printers and typewriters.

SPECIAL SERVICES FOR THE HANDICAPPED
Elevator access if necessary; Visualtek Large Print Display Processor (machine to enlarge print for the visually impaired).

SIZE OF COLLECTIONS/HOLDINGS

GENERAL
The Mina Rees Library has over 185,000 bound volumes, including monographs and serials, 328,000 microfilms, and 145,000 art slides.There are approximately 1600 serial publications, including journals.

LATIN AMERICAN
In the broad area of Latin American studies, the Mina Rees Library has approximately 5,500 volumes. Approximately 3,400 are in the Spanish language and 100 in the Portuguese language. There are approximately 75 periodicals, most of which are in literature.

DESCRIPTION AND EVALUATION OF COLLECTIONS

LATIN AMERICAN HOLDINGS
The Graduate School/CUNY does not currently offer a degree program in Latin American studies; monographs and serials in Latin American studies are acquired as necessary, in support of course work in the social sciences and humanities. Monographs in the social sciences are often in English translation, although the Latin American literature collection is generally in Spanish.

EVALUATION OF
SUBJECT/AREA STRENGTH

Refer to page 110 for definitions of collection rating levels.

Subject Category		Collection Rating Level (A-E)	
		Monographs	Serials
1.	Bibliography & Reference	A	A
2.	Economics	A	A
3.	Education	-	-
4.	Geography & Anthropology	B	B
5.	History	B	B
6.	International Relations	A	A
7.	Language & Literature	C	C
8.	Law	-	-
9.	Military Affairs	A	A
10.	Philosophy & Religion	A	A
11.	Politics & Government	B	B
12.	Sociology	B	B

SPECIAL COLLECTIONS

GOVERNMENT DOCUMENTS
Selected U.S. federal documents. No systematically collected documents from federal, state, municipal or foreign governments.

ARCHIVES AND MANUSCRIPTS
Archives only of Graduate School & University Center records and publications.

PROMINENT COLLECTIONS, RARE BOOKS, ETC.
Human Relations Area Files (HRAF).

HARRY A. SPRAGUE LIBRARY
Montclair State College
Upper Montclair, NJ 07043
(201) 893-4297

GENERAL INFORMATION

HOURS OF SERVICE
7:30 a.m. to 10:00 p.m., Monday through Thursday; 7:30 a.m. to 4:30 p.m., Friday; 10:30 a.m. to 4:30 p.m., Saturday; 1:00 p.m. to 9:00 p.m., Sunday.

CONDITIONS OF ACCESS
Open to all adults for in-house use. Borrowing restricted to college community.

COOPERATIVE ARRANGEMENTS WITH OTHER INSTITUTIONS
METRO (practically all libraries public, special and academic in New York); NJALN; Senior Public College Libraries in New Jersey; interlibrary loan with U.S. and Canadian libraries.

FACILITIES
Photocopiers, microreaders and reader-printers, TV, listening equipment of many types, video cassette and other viewing equipment.

SPECIAL SERVICES FOR THE HANDICAPPED
Entrance and egress, special door, elevator.

SIZE OF COLLECTIONS/HOLDINGS

GENERAL
357,765 bound volumes; 73,612 government documents (microforms); 30,917 government documents; 804,197 microforms (items); 40,875 non-print media, other (items); total collection 1,307,366 items.

LATIN AMERICAN
Books: history: 2,700; literature: 3,100; political science: 150; linguistics: 200; economics: 400; others (estimate): 800; total books: 7,350. Estimate of relevant periodical titles: 50.

DESCRIPTION AND EVALUATION OF COLLECTION

LATIN AMERICAN HOLDINGS
The Library has a study-level book collection with particular strengths in history and literature. The periodical collection is on a basic level with a few of the major periodicals, mostly on literature.

EVALUATION OF SUBJECT/AREA STRENGTH

Refer to page 110 for definitions of collection rating levels.

Subject Category		Collection Rating Level (A-E)	
		Monographs	Serials
1.	Bibliography & Reference	A	A
2.	Economics	B	A
3.	Education	A	A
4.	Geography & Anthropology	B	A
5.	History	B	A
6.	International Relations	A	A
7.	Language & Literature	B	A
8.	Law	A	A
9.	Military Affairs	A	A
10.	Philosophy & Religion	A	A
11.	Politics & Government	A	A
12.	Sociology	A	A

Area Category		Monographs	Serials
13.	Argentina	B	A
14.	Belize	A	A
15.	Bolivia	A	A
16.	Brazil	B	A
17.	Caribbean (excl. Cuba)	A	A
18.	Chile	A	A
19.	Colombia	A	A
20.	Costa Rica	A	A
21.	Cuba	B	A
22.	Dominican Republic	A	A
23.	Ecuador	A	A
24.	El Salvador	A	A
25.	Guatemala	A	A
26.	Guianas	A	A
27.	Haiti	A	A
28.	Honduras	A	A
29.	Jamaica	A	A
30.	Mexico	B	A
31.	Nicaragua	A	A
32.	Panama	A	A
33.	Paraguay	A	A
34.	Peru	A	A
35.	Uruguay	A	A
36.	Venezuela	A	A
37.	Other	A	A

SPECIAL COLLECTIONS

GOVERNMENT DOCUMENTS
The Library is a selected U.S. Government Documents Depository and a New Jersey State Documents Depository.

FILMS/TAPES
25 videocassettes; 6 filmstrips; 6 audiotapes and records; 2 slide sets.

PROMINENT COLLECTIONS, RARE BOOKS, ETC.
There is some unusual material in Portuguese on various subjects such as geography, literature and history.

THE WALL STREET JOURNAL LIBRARY
World Financial Center 200 Liberty Street
New York, NY 10281
(212) 416-2676

201

GENERAL INFORMATION

HOURS OF SERVICE
9:00 a.m. to 5:00 p.m., Monday through Friday.

CONDITIONS OF ACCESS
Access by telephone only. Photocopies of articles are available by written request (include $1.00 per article).

JACQUELINE WEXLER LIBRARY
Hunter College
of the City University of New York
695 Park Avenue
New York, NY 10021
(212) 772-4146

202

GENERAL INFORMATION

CONDITIONS OF ACCESS
Not open to the general public. All CUNY students and faculty have access. Member of METRO.

COOPERATIVE ARRANGEMENTS WITH OTHER INSTITUTIONS
Member of METRO.

FACILITIES
Reproduction equipment, typewriters, microreaders, etc. are available.

SPECIAL SERVICES FOR THE HANDICAPPED
Visual-Tek, talking calculators and large print typewriters are available.

SIZE OF COLLECTIONS/HOLDINGS

GENERAL
About 600,000 volumes; c. 3500 periodicals.

LATIN AMERICAN
About 7000 volumes, primarily in literature and history.

DESCRIPTION AND EVALUATION OF COLLECTION

LATIN AMERICAN HOLDINGS
The collection has reasonable depth for undergraduate study. Recent improvements have been made; however more is being selected in literature than other areas.

EVALUATION OF   Refer to page 110 for definitions
SUBJECT/AREA STRENGTH   of collection rating levels.

Subject Category		Collection Rating Level (A-E)	
		Monographs	Serials
1.	Bibliography & Reference	B	A
2.	Economics	A	A
3.	Education	A	A
4.	Geography & Anthropology	A	A
5.	History	A	A
6.	International Relations	A	A
7.	Language & Literature	B	B
8.	Law	A	A
9.	Military Affairs	A	A
10.	Philosophy & Religion	A	A
11.	Politics & Government	A	A
12.	Sociology	A	A

Area Category		Monographs	Serials
13.	Argentina	A	A
14.	Belize	A	A
15.	Bolivia	A	A
16.	Brazil	B	A
17.	Caribbean (excl. Cuba)	B	A
18.	Chile	A	A
19.	Colombia	A	A
20.	Costa Rica	A	A
21.	Cuba	A	A
22.	Dominican Republic	A	A
23.	Ecuador	A	A
24.	El Salvador	A	A
25.	Guatemala	A	A
26.	Guianas	A	A
27.	Haiti	A	A
28.	Honduras	A	A
29.	Jamaica	A	A
30.	Mexico	A	A
31.	Nicaragua	A	A
32.	Panama	A	A
33.	Paraguay	A	A
34.	Peru	A	A
35.	Uruguay	A	A
36.	Venezuela	A	A
37.	Other	A	-

UNITED NATIONS AGENCIES

The following information was requested for each entry in this section. However, final entries contain only those categories which each organization deemed applicable.

Identification:
  - Name
  - Address
  - Telephone

Conditions of access

Functions, programs, research activities

Libraries and reference facilities

Publications

UNITED NATIONS ARCHIVES
345 Park Avenue South
New York, NY 10010
(212) 963-2939

CONDITIONS OF ACCESS
Archival records are open for research when they are more than 20 years old and not subject to restrictions imposed by the Secretary General.

FUNCTIONS, PROGRAMS, RESEARCH ACTIVITIES
The UN Archives is responsible for the custody, preservation and servicing of the archival materials and records of the United Nations that should be preserved because of their administrative, legal, historical or other value as evidence of the official business of the United Nations. It is also responsible for the archives and records of the Secretariat Units away from Headquarters and for the subsidiary organizations of the United Nations.

LIBRARIES/REFERENCE FACILITIES
Archival materials pertaining to Latin America and the Caribbean are dispersed over the entire holdings, i.e., some 30 archives groups organized according to the provenance principle. There are no collections or holdings based on geographical lines.

UNITED NATIONS CENTER
FOR SCIENCE AND TECHNOLOGY
FOR DEVELOPMENT
One United Nations Plaza, Room DC1-1022
New York, NY 10017
(212) 963-8807

CONDITIONS OF ACCESS
For publications: United Nations Bookshop, Room Ga-032A, United Nations Secretariat Building (tel.: 754-7680) public sales; documents made available to universities and nonprofit organizations at their request.

FUNCTIONS, PROGRAMS, RESEARCH ACTIVITIES
The Centre is in charge of the following functions in the area of science and technology for development: monitoring, coordinating and reviewing of joint activities by United Nations agencies; research and analysis of national policies and liaison with national policy-making centers and nongovernmental organizations. The activities undertaken focus mainly on developing countries. In the case of Latin

American countries, the Centre cooperates closely with the Economic Commission for Latin America and the Caribbean, located in Santiago, Chile. New and current programs include: information systems on science and technology for development; technology applied to agricultural development and related development areas; mobilization of resources for science and technology; application of science and technology to the study, prevention, monitoring and combatting of drought, desertification and other natural disasters; impact of new and emerging areas of science and technology on the development of developing countries.

LIBRARIES/REFERENCE FACILITIES
The Centre uses the services of the Dag Hammarskjöld Library of the United Nations.

PUBLICATIONS
Periodical publications: *UPDATE:* Magazine of general information; *ATAS: Advance Technology Alert System Bulletin; Annual Registry of National Focal Points of Science and Technology for Development.* Reports on regional meetings: Structures for science and technology policy formulation and implementation in Latin America and the Caribbean; documents such as: 1) *Latin America and the Vienna Program of Action: Science and Technology for Development in the 1980s;* 2) *Report of the Ninth Session of the Committee of High-Level Government Experts: Science and Technology for Development* (Economic Commission for Latin America). Sales publications covering meeting proceedings include: *Science and Technology Indicators for Development; Trends and Prospects in Planning and Management of Science and Technology for Development; Research and Development: Linkages to Production in Developing Countries.*

 UNITED NATIONS CENTRE ON TRANSNATIONAL CORPORATIONS (UNCTC)
United Nations
New York, NY 10017
(212) 963-3176

CONDITIONS OF ACCESS
Facilities available to governments and intergovernmental organizations, and to others as resources permit.

FUNCTIONS, PROGRAMS, RESEARCH ACTIVITIES
UNCTC serves as secretariat to the Commission on Transnational Corporations, an intergovernmental subsidiary body of the United Nations Economic and Social Council. The objectives of the work program are to further the understanding of

the nature of transnational corporations and of their political, legal, economic and social effects on home and host countries; to secure effective international arrangements aimed at enhancing the contribution of transnational corporations to national development goals and world economic growth while controlling and eliminating their negative effects; and to strengthen the negotiating capacity of host countries in their dealings with transnational corporations.

The work program includes the provision of assistance to the Commission on Transnational Corporations in securing an effective code of conduct and other international arrangements and agreements relating to transnational corporations and conducting research and analyses on general trends in the nature and extent of the operations of transnational corporations; on measures strengthening the negotiating capacity of governments in their relations with transnational corporations; on the political, social and cultural impact of transnational corporations on host developing countries; and on the activities of transnational corporations in specific areas and selected sectors.

In addition, UNCTC provides advisory and information services and training services to developing countries aimed at enhancing their negotiating capabilities with transnational corporations and operates an information system on transnational corporations. UNCTC has joint units with each of the regional commissions of the United Nations, including one with the Economic Commission for Latin America and the Caribbean.

LIBRARIES/REFERENCE FACILITIES
UNCTC has a small library with a collection that focuses on transnational corporations. The library may be consulted by appointment. Response is also provided to inquiries received by mail and telephone as resources permit.

UNITED NATIONS CHILDREN'S FUND (UNICEF) 206
3 United Nations Plaza
New York, NY 10017
(212) 326-7000

FUNCTIONS, PROGRAMS, RESEARCH ACTIVITIES
UNICEF pursues its advocacy role on behalf of children in both industrialized and developing countries. As an integral, semiautonomous part of the UN, UNICEF comprises a network of country and regional offices serving 118 countries in the developing world, supported by national committees and other voluntary organizations in the industrialized world. Through its country offices, UNICEF cooperates with governments in their efforts to meet the needs of children, gearing the cooperation to the particular situation and priorities, with relatively greater support for the least developed nations and particular attention to the major causes of

death and disease among children under five. Advocacy and action focus on the world's high levels of infant and young child death and disease. UNICEF's approach is on self-reliant community-based services as the practical, organized foundation on which the possibility of a virtual revolution in child survival and development is based.

UNICEF not only seeks government and public support for programs of cooperation but also tries to stimulate public awareness of children's needs and the means to meet them by advocacy–with governments, civic leaders, educators and other professional and cultural groups, the media and local communities. UNICEF's programs cover the following major areas: nutrition; social services; water and sanitation; primary health care; formal and nonformal education for mothers and children; emergency relief and rehabilitation; planning and project support.

PUBLICATIONS
UNICEF publishes an *Annual Report* and other activity related reports and brochures. Other materials available include videotapes and films.

UNITED NATIONS DEPARTMENT OF INTERNATIONAL ECONOMIC AND SOCIAL AFFAIRS
Office for Development Research and Policy Analysis
2 United Nations Plaza, Room 2002
New York, NY 10017
(212) 963-4744

FUNCTIONS, PROGRAMS, RESEARCH ACTIVITIES
Research on Latin America exists largely when it is a relevant input to the *World Economic Survey* (annual publication). For basic data, considerable reliance on Economic Commission for Latin America and the Caribbean and national sources. Studies on Latin America are also undertaken as input to other reports of the Department requested by the Economic and Social Council and the General Assembly, such as the ones on debt, on net transfer of resources, on money, trade and finance.

LIBRARIES/REFERENCE FACILITIES
Small reference unit for internal use only; Dag Hammarskjöld Library, United Nations; Statistical Office Library–Department of International Economic and Social Affairs.

PUBLICATIONS

World Economic Survey (annual, appears in June); *Report on the World Social Situation* (every four years); *Journal of Development Planning;* reports as requested by the General Assembly, e.g., *International Debt Situation in mid-1986* (Report of the Secretary-General, UN document A/41/643, 1 October 1986); *International Cooperation in the Fields of Money, Finance, Debt, Resource Flows, Trade and Development* (Report of the Secretary-General, UN document A/C.2/40/15, 16 April 1986); *International Cooperation in the Fields of Money, Finance, Debt, Resource Flows, Trade and Development* (Report of the Secretary-General, UN document A/40/708, 11 October 1985); *Net Transfer of Resources from Developing to Developed Countries* (Report of the Secretary-General, UN document E/1987/72 and A/42/272).

UNITED NATIONS DEPARTMENT OF TECHNICAL COOPERATION FOR DEVELOPMENT

One United Nations Plaza
New York, NY 10017
(212) 963-8362

FUNCTIONS, PROGRAMS, RESEARCH ACTIVITIES

The Department of Technical Cooperation for Development is the operational arm of the United Nations Secretariat for the execution of technical cooperation projects in developing countries in the following fields: natural resources and energy; development planning; public administration; population and statistics.

The Department publishes reports on projects, and other reports and papers related to its work, including proceedings of meetings, conferences and seminars.

LIBRARIES/RESEARCH FACILITIES

Many of the Department's publications are available. Consult the Department.

PUBLICATIONS

Project reports are available in the Department's Reports Unit and are of two types: technical reports, which are highly technical in nature and are aimed at experts, and agency terminal reports, which are descriptive and historical and are aimed at laymen, particularly decisionmakers and policymakers. Only those project reports which have been derestricted may be consulted.

Natural Resources publications are available through the United Nations Sales
Section and, for consultation, in the Natural Resources Reference Centre:

Natural Resources Reference Centre
Natural Resources and Energy Division
Department of Technical Cooperation for Development
United Nations, New York, NY 10017
(212) 754-8764

The Department also publishes the *Natural Resources Forum*, a quarterly publication; subscriptions are available through:

Graham and Trotman
Sterling House
66 Wilton Road
London, England SW1V 1DE

 UNITED NATIONS
DEVELOPMENT FUND FOR WOMEN
(UNIFEM)
304 East 45th Street
New York, NY 10017
(212) 906-6435

CONDITIONS OF ACCESS
Governments and nongovernmental organizations can submit applications for
support through their country office of the United Nations Development Program
(UNDP).

FUNCTIONS, PROGRAMS, RESEARCH ACTIVITIES
UNIFEM supports activities which directly assist women and help them to become
self-reliant. In addition, income-generating projects which also help women use
the income to benefit themselves, their families and their communities. The five
major sectors are: Development Planning, Project Implementation, Income Gen-
erating Activities, New and Renewable Energy Technologies, Water Supplies,
Rural Development (Agriculture/Fishing), Urban Development (Industrialization/
Import Substitution), Training of Trainers/Leaders, Volunteer Service (Technical
Cooperation among Developing Countries) and Information/Communication.

Activities are of two main types: a) programming missions of a preinvestment nature to determine technical feasibility, or advice on directing mainstream resources so that women are taken into account; b) operational programs with direct immediate benefits. These programs are generally innovative and often experim-

ental. They tend to strengthen self-sustaining activities among groups of women aimed at long-term and income-generating multiplier effects. Types of assistance under each category include: employment/training, human development, development planning, energy technologies, water supplies, urban/rural development and information/communication.

PUBLICATIONS
The Fund publishes several brochures covering the most recent information on Fund projects and activities, its history, credit fund information, achievements, guides and reports. Other materials available include sound/slide sets, and a film focusing on a small business enterprise project in Colombia.

UNITED NATIONS DEVELOPMENT PROGRAMME (UNDP)
Regional Bureau for Latin America and the Caribbean
One United Nations Plaza
New York, NY 10017
(212) 906-5400

210

CONDITIONS OF ACCESS
Limited. By appointment only.

FUNCTIONS, PROGRAMS, RESEARCH ACTIVITIES
The United Nations Development Program (UNDP) is the world's largest channel for multilateral technical and preinvestment cooperation. It is active in some 150 countries and territories and in virtually every economic and social sector, including farming, fishing, forestry, mining, manufacturing, power, transport, communications, housing and building, trade and tourism, health and environmental sanitation, education and training, community development, economic planning and public administration.

There are more than 5,000 UNDP-supported projects currently in operation, at the regional, national, interregional and global levels, aimed at helping developing countries make better use of their assets, improve living standards and expand productivity. These projects involve: (a) carrying out surveys and feasibility studies to determine the availability and economic value of a developing country's natural resources and to assess other potentials for increased output and wider distribution of goods and services; (b) helping to mobilize the capital investments required to realize these potentials; (c) expanding and strengthening educational systems from primary through university levels, and supporting a full spectrum of professional, vocational and technical instruction, from work-oriented literacy training to the provision of fellowships for specialized studies abroad; (d) establishing facilities for applying modern technological research methods to priority development problems and for disseminating new discoveries and production techniques; and (e) upgrading capabilities for economic and social development planning.

In all these areas, the UNDP works to broaden economic and technical cooperation among the developing countries themselves.

UNDP assistance is rendered only at the request of governments and in response to their priority needs, integrated into overall national and regional plans. Almost all projects are carried out by one of the United Nations-related agencies and programs.

The UNDP also administers a number of special purpose funds and programs, including: the United Nations Capital Development Fund, which provides grants and long-term loans for grassroots self-help activities in some of the world's poorest countries; the United Nations Revolving Fund for Natural Resources Exploration, which helps developing countries carry out potentially high-return mineral searches that they cannot afford on their own; the United Nations Sudano-Sahelian Office; the United Nations Volunteers; and the United Nations Financing System for Science and Technology for Development.

The UNDP is financed by voluntary contributions from Member States of the United Nations and its related agencies.

Offices are maintained in 24 countries throughout Latin America and the Caribbean.

PUBLICATIONS
Numerous free-of-charge booklets, audio visuals and periodicals on general information on the UNDP, its affiliated UN organizations and its special projects are available. Among these are official reports on field services delivered, programs, management and financing, technical cooperation, method evaluation; worldwide or multiregional scale projects, including research on food crops and plant and livestock pest and disease control, campaigns to combat diseases; water and sanitation systems, employment-generating rural work programs, multilateral development cooperation and educational activities.

UNITED NATIONS FUND FOR POPULATION ACTIVITIES (UNFPA)
Latin America and Caribbean Branch
220 East 42nd Street (DN-1800)
New York, NY 10017
(212) 850-5689/5690

211

CONDITIONS OF ACCESS
Open to the public.

FUNCTIONS, PROGRAMS, RESEARCH ACTIVITIES
UNFPA provides support to governments and nongovernmental organizations for population activities including family planning, communication and education, basic data collection, population dynamics, formulation and evaluation of population policies and programs, implementation of policies and programs, special programs, e.g., women, children and youth, the aged, and multisector activities, e.g., population conferences, documentation centers, clearing houses, interdisciplinary training.

LIBRARIES/REFERENCE FACILITIES
Open to qualified researchers and students.

PUBLICATIONS
A monthly newsletter, *Population,* is available on request in Spanish and English. General information leaflets, special reports, periodicals, conference reports, monographs and reference books are available. In addition, books issued by other publishers may be ordered directly from the publisher. Films may be purchased and/or loaned. The following are some of the topics treated by UNFPA's publications: population policies (family planning, food problems, distribution and development, aging), demographics, regional and national population situations and population programs and projects.

UNITED NATIONS INSTITUTE FOR TRAINING AND RESEARCH (UNITAR)
801 United Nations Plaza
New York, NY 10017
(212) 963-8622

212

FUNCTIONS, PROGRAMS, RESEARCH ACTIVITIES
The two functions of UNITAR are training and research.

UNITAR provides training at various levels to persons, particularly from developing countries, for assignments in the United Nations or the specialized agencies and for assignment in their national organizations related to it, or other institutions operating in related fields. Training activities include training for international cooperation and multilateral diplomacy and for economic and social development.

UNITAR conducts research and study related to the functions and objectives of the United Nations, giving appropriate priority to the requirements of the Secretary-General of the United Nations and of other United Nations organs and the specialized agencies. Research activities include research on the United Nations and on issues of concern to it, particularly peace and security issues, economic and social development, institutional issues concerning the adequacy of the United Nations system to achieve its objectives and on the future of the main developing regions of the world.

PUBLICATIONS
UNITAR books and periodicals are available from United Nations Publications Sales Section. Some publications are available from commercial publishers. Recent titles on Latin America include: G. Martner/Coord.: *América Latina hacia el 2000 . Opciones y Estrategias* (1986); E. Faletto, G. Martner/Coord.: *Repensar el Futuro – Estilos de Desarrollo* (1986); *Venezuela hacia el 2000. Desafíos y Opciones* (1987); *Costa Rica hacia el 2000. Desafíos y Opciones* (1987); *México hacia el 2000. Desafíos y Opciones* (1987); *Argentina hacia el 2000. Desafíos y Opciones* (1987).

BOOKSTORES AND PUBLISHING HOUSES

B. DALTON
666 Fifth Avenue, New York, NY 10019
(212) 247-1740

BARNES & NOBLE
105 Fifth Avenue, New York, NY 10003
(212) 807-0099

BOOKFORUM
2955 Broadway, New York, NY 10025
(212) 749-5535

CITY COLLEGE BOOKSTORE
138th Street & Convent Avenue, New York, NY 10031
(212) 368-4000

COLUMBIA UNIVERSITY BOOKSTORE
2926 Broadway, New York, NY 10027
(212) 866-8210

EDICIONES VITRAL
P.O. Box 20043, Greely Square Station, New York, NY 10001

EL CASCAJERO
506 West Broadway, New York, NY 10012
(212) 254-0905

ELISEO TORRES SPANISH AND PORTUGUESE BOOK CENTER
1164 Garrison Avenue, Bronx, NY 10474
(212) 589-8300

THE FEMINIST PRESS
311 East 94th Street, New York, NY 10128
(212) 360-5790

THE FRENCH AND SPANISH BOOK CORPORATION
115 Fifth Avenue, New York, NY 10003
(212) 673-7400

GROVE PRESS, INC.
196 West Houston Street, New York, NY 10014
(212) 529-3600

LAS AMERICAS
911 Faile Street, Bronx, NY 10459
(212) 893-4445

LECTORUM PUBLICATIONS, INC.
137 West 14th Street, New York, NY 10011
(212) 929-2833

LIBERATION BOOKSTORE
421 Lenox Avenue, New York, NY 10037
(212) 281-4615

LA LIBRAIRIE DE FRANCE
610 Fifth Avenue, New York, NY 10020
(212) 581-8810

LUSO-BRAZILIAN BOOKS
P.O. Box 286, Times Plaza Station, Brooklyn, NY 11217
(718) 624-4000

MACONDO BOOKS INC.
221 West 14th Street, New York, NY 10011
(212) 741-3108

MADISON AVENUE BOOKSHOP
833 Madison Avenue, New York, NY 10021
(212) 535-6130

MONTHLY REVIEW PRESS
155 West 23rd Street,12th Floor, New York, NY 10011
(212) 691-2555

NATIONAL BOOKSTORES
15 Astor Place, New York, NY 10021
(212) 475-4946

NEW DIRECTIONS
80 Eighth Avenue, New York, NY 10011
(212) 255-0230

NEW YORK UNIVERSITY BOOKSTORE
18 Washington Place, New York, NY 10012
(212) 998-2259

PAPYRUS BOOKSELLERS
2915 Broadway, New York, NY 10015
(212) 222-3350

PENINSULA PUBLISHING CO.
156 Fifth Avenue, Room 617, New York, NY 10010
(212) 645-6128

REVOLUTION BOOKS
13 East 16th Street, New York, NY 10003
(212) 691-3345

ST. MARK'S BOOKSHOP
13 St. Mark's Place, New York, NY 10003
(212) 260-7853

STRAND BOOKSTORE
828 Broadway, New York, NY 10003
(212) 473-1452

UNITED NATIONS BOOKSHOP
General Assembly Building, Room GA32B, New York, Y 10017
(212) 754-7680

UNITED STATES GOVERNMENT BOOKSTORE
26 Federal Plaza, Room 110, New York, NY 10278
(212) 264-3826

UNITY BOOK CENTER
235 West 23rd Street, New York, NY 10011
(212) 242-2934

UNIVERSITY PLACE BOOKSHOP
821 Broadway, New York, NY 10003
(212) 254-5998

WALDEN BOOKSTORES
57 Broadway, New York, NY 10006
(212) 269-1139

WOMANBOOKS
656 Amsterdam Avenue, New York, NY 10025
(212) 873-4121

PUBLICATIONS & MEDIA

AMSTERDAM NEWS
2340 Eighth Avenue, New York, NY 10027
(212) 678-6600

CHALLENGE-DESAFIO
2211 Church Avenue, Room 210, Brooklyn, NY 11226
(718) 282-9000

DAILY NEWS
220 East 42nd Street, New York, NY 10017
(212) 210-2100

EL DIARIO-LA PRENSA
143 Varick, New York, NY 10013
(212) 807- 4600

INTERNATIONAL REPORTS
14 East 60th Street, Suite 1206, New York, NY 10022
(212) 477-0003

INTERPRESS SERVICE NEWS AGENCY
777 United Nations Plaza, New York, NY 10017
(212) 286-0123

JOHNSTON INTERNATIONAL PUBLISHING CORPORATION
386 Park Avenue South, New York, NY 10016
(212) 689-0120

LAGNIAPPE LETTER & LAGNIAPPE QUARTERLY REPORT
222 Central Park South, New York, NY 10019
(212) 586-6498

MEDIA NETWORK
121 Fulton, New York, NY 10011
(212) 619-3455

THE NATION
72 Fifth Avenue, New York, NY 10011
(212) 242-8400

NATIONAL FILM BOARD OF CANADA
1251 Avenue of the Americas, New York, NY 10020
(212) 586-5131

NATIONAL FILM CENTER
232 East 46th Street, New York, NY 10017
(212) 279-2000

NATIONAL LAW JOURNAL
111 Eighth Avenue, New York, NY 10011
(212) 741-8300

NATIONAL NEWS COUNCIL
1 Lincoln Plaza, New York, NY 10023
(212) 595-9411

NATIONAL NEWS SERVICE
5 Beekman Street, New York, NY 10038
(212) 344-4242

NATIONAL PUBLIC RADIO
New York News Bureau
801 Second Avenue, New York, NY 10017
(212) 490-2444

NEWSDAY
235 Pinelawn Road, Melville, NY 11747
(516) 454-2550

NEWSWEEK
444 Madison Avenue, New York, NY 10022
(212) 350-4000

THE NEW YORK TIMES
229 West 43rd Street, New York, NY 10036
(212) 556-1234

NOTICIAS DEL MUNDO
401 Fifth Avenue, 40th Floor, New York, NY 10036
(212) 576-0370

THIRD WORLD NEWSREEL
335 West 38th Street, 5th Floor, New York, NY 10018
(212) 947-9277

EL TIEMPO DE NUEVA YORK
37-37 88th Street, Jackson Heights, NY 11372
(718) 507-0832

TIME MAGAZINE
Time & Life Building
Rockefeller Center, New York, NY 10020
(212) 586-1212

U.S. NEWS AND WORLD REPORT
45 Rockefeller Plaza, New York, NY 10020
(212) 246-3366

VILLAGE VOICE
842 Broadway, New York, NY 10003
(212) 475-3300

VOICE OF AMERICA
26 Federal Plaza, Room 30-100, New York, NY 10278
(212) 264-2345

LA VOZ HISPANA
159 East 116th Street, New York, NY 10029
(212) 348-2100

WALL STREET JOURNAL
200 Liberty Street, New York, NY 10281
(212) 416-2000

TINKER GUIDE TO
CITY UNIVERSITY OF NEW YORK
SCHOLARS OF LATIN AMERICAN
AND CARIBBEAN AFFAIRS

1. Mexico Scholars

BYLAND, BRUCE
1. Mexico
2. Anthropology
3. Herbert H. Lehman College
   Bedford Park Blvd. West
   Bronx, NY 10468
   (212) 960-8405/8128

EDEL, MATTHEW
1. Mexico
2. Economics & Urban Studies
3. Queens College &GSUC
   65-30 Kissena Blvd.
   Flushing, NY 11367
   (718) 520-7530

HASLIP-VIERA, GABRIEL
1. Mexico
2. History
3. City College
   Convent Avenue
   & 138th Street
   New York, NY 10031
   (212) 690-6763

HOFFMAN, JOAN
1. Mexico
2. Economics
3. John Jay College
   444 West 56th Street
   New York, NY 10019
   (212) 489-5011

HU-DEHART, EVELYN
1. Mexico
2. History
3. Herbert H. Lehman College
   & GSUC
   Bedford Park Blvd. West
   Bronx, NY 10468
   (212) 960-8289/8288

LEES, SUSAN
1. Mexico
2. Anthropology
3. Hunter College
   695 Park Ave.
   New York, NY 10021
   (212) 570-5758

NASH, JUNE
1. Mexico
2. Anthropology
3. City College & GSUC
   Convent Ave. & 138th Street
   New York, NY 10031
   (212) 690-6608/8162

PACHON, HARRY
1. Mexico
2. Public Administration &
   Political Science
3. Bernard M. Baruch College
   17 Lexington Ave.
   New York, NY 10010
   (212) 725-3375

RANDALL, LAURA
1. Mexico
2. Economics
3. Hunter College
   695 Park Ave.
   New York, NY 10021
   (212) 772-5400

SUSS, STUART
1. Mexico
2. History
3. Kingsborough Community College
   2001 Oriental Blvd.
   Brooklyn, NY 11235
   (718) 934-5170

WATERBURY, RONALD
1. Mexico
2. Anthropology
3. Queens College
   65-30 Kissena Blvd.
   Flushing, NY 11367
   (718) 520-7046

WHITE, RUSSELL
1. Mexico
2. Geography
3. Hunter College
   695 Park Ave.
   New York, NY 10021
   (212) 772-5265

WOLF, ERIC
1. Mexico
2. Anthropology
3. Herbert H. Lehman College
   Bedford Park Blvd. West
   Bronx, NY 10468
   (212) 960-8518

2. Central American and Caribbean Scholars

ARROYO, GILBERTO
1. Puerto Rico
2. Economics
3. LaGuardia Community College
   31-10 Thomson Ave.
   Long Island City, NY 11101
   (212) 626-5540

BAVER, SHERRIE
1. Puerto Rico
2. Political Science
3. City College
   Convent Ave. & 138th Street
   New York, NY 10031
   (212) 690-6763

BENDIX, EDWARD
1. Caribbean
2. Anthropology
3. Hunter College & GSUC
   695 Park Ave.
   New York, NY 10021
   (212) 570-5758

BERGAD, LAIRD
1. Caribbean
2. History
3. Herbert H. Lehman College
   Bedford Park Blvd. West
   Bronx, NY 10468
   (212) 960-8280

BERNSTEIN, RICHARD
1. Dominican Republic
2. General Internal Medicine
3. Mt. Sinai School of Medicine
   1 Gustave L. Levy Place
   New York, NY 10029
   (212) 650-7612

BONILLA, FRANK
1. Puerto Rico
2. Sociology
3. Hunter College & GSUC
   695 Park Ave.
   New York, NY 10021
   (212) 772-5585

BONNETT, AUBREY
1. Caribbean
2. Sociology
3. Hunter College
   695 Park Ave.
   New York, NY 10021
   (212) 772-5585

BOSCH, SAMUEL J.
1. Dominican Republic
2. International Community Medicine
3. Mt. Sinai School of Medicine
   1 Gustave L. Levy Place
   New York, NY 10029
   (212) 650-7941

BRAVEBOY-WAGNER, JACQUELINE
1. Caribbean
2. Political Science
3. City College
   Convent Ave. & 138th Street
   New York, NY 10031
   (212) 690- 5470

BRYCE LA PORTE, ROY SIMON
1. Panama, Caribbean and
Central America
2. Sociology
3. College of Staten Island & GSUC
130 Stuyvessant Place
Staten Island, NY 10301
(718) 390-7946

BYLAND, BRUCE
1. Belize
2. Anthropology
3. Herbert H. Lehman College
   Bedford Park Blvd. West
   Bronx, NY 10468
   (212) 960-8405/8128

CRESPO, OLIVER
1. Dominican Republic
2. Psychology
3. Hostos Community College
   475 Grand Concourse
   Bronx, NY 10451

DAWES, HUGH
1. Jamaica
2. Economics
3. Manhattan Community College
   199 Chambers Street
   New York, NY 10007
   (212) 618-1383

DEUSCHLE, KURT W.
1. Dominican Republic, Jamaica
2. International Community Medicine
3. Mt. Sinai School of Medicine
   1 Gustave L. Levy Place
   New York, NY 10029
   (212) 650-7831

DIAZ, MICHÆL
1. Dominican Republic
2. Emergency Care
3. Mt. Sinai School of Medicine
   1 Gustave L. Levy Place
   New York, NY 10029
   (212) 772-3860

EDEL, MATTHEW
1. Caribbean
2. Economics and Urban Studies
2. Queens College & GSUC
   65-30 Kissena Blvd.
   Flushing, NY 11367
   (718) 520-7530

ELIJOVICH, FERNANDO
1. Spanish-speaking Caribbean
2. General Internal Medicine
3. Mt. Sinai School of Medicine
   1 Gustave L. Levy Place
   New York, NY 10029
   (212) 650-7840

FAHS, MARIANNE
1. English-speaking Caribbean
2. Health Economics
3. Mt. Sinai School of Medicine
   1 Gustave L. Levy Place
   New York, NY 10029
   (212) 650-7840

FARBER, SAMUEL
1. Cuba
2. Political Science
3. Brooklyn College
   Bedford Ave. & Ave. H
   Brooklyn, NY 11210
   (718) 780-5627

FARQUHAR, DAVID
1. Caribbean
2. History
3. Manhattan Community College
   199 Chambers Street
   New York, NY 10007
   (212) 618-1424

FISCHER, ELLEN
1. Dominican Republic
2. Epidemiology
3. Mt. Sinai School of Medicine
   1 Gustave L. Levy Place
   New York, NY 10029
   (212) 650-7700

FLORES, JUAN
1. Puerto Rico
2. Sociology
3. Queens College
   65-30 Kissena Blvd.
   Flushing, NY 11367
   (718) 520-7088

FREIDENBERG, JUDITH
1. Latin America & the Caribbean
2. Anthropology
3. Mt. Sinai School of Medicine
   1 Gustave L. Levy Place
   New York, NY 10029
   (212)- 650-7852/46

GERASSI, JOHN
1. Nicaragua
2. Political Science
3. Queens College
   65-30 Kissena Blvd.
   Flushing, NY 11367
   (718) 520-7373

HAMMOND, JACK
1. Central America
2. Sociology
3. Hunter College & GSUC
   695 Park Ave.
   New York, NY 10021
   (212) 772-5573

HASLIP-VIERA, GABRIEL
1. Caribbean
2. History
3. City College
   Convent Ave. & 138th Street
   New York, NY 10031
   (212) 690-6763

HELLMAN, RONALD G.
1. Costa Rica
2. Sociology & Political Science
3. Graduate School
   33 West 42nd Street
   New York, NY 10036
   (212) 382-2047

IRIZARRY, JOSE E.
1. Caribbean
2. History
3. City College
   Convent Ave. & 138th Street
   New York, NY 10031
   (212) 690-6763

JERVIS, JAMES
1. Caribbean
2. History & Sociology
3. Herbert H. Lehman College
   Bedford Park Blvd. West
   Bronx, NY 10468
   (212) 960-8283

JULIUS, NADINE
1. English-speaking Caribbean
2. Community Social Work
3. Mt. Sinai School of Medicine
   1 Gustave L. Levy Place
   New York, NY 10029
   (212) 650-7940

KINSBRUNER, JAY
1. Caribbean
2. History
3. Queens College & GSUC
   65-30 Kissena Blvd.
   Flushing, NY 11367
   (718) 520-7364

LARAQUE, FRANCK
1. Haiti, Cuba
2. Political Science
3. City College
   Convent Ave. & 138th Street
   New York, NY 10031
   (212) 690-8117

LEWIN, ARTHUR
1. Jamaica
2. Sociology
3. Bernard M. Baruch College
   17 Lexington Ave.
   New York, NY 10010
   (212) 725-3324

LEWIS, WILLIAM
1. Jamaica
2. Anthropology
3. John Jay College
   444 West 56th Street
   New York, NY 10019
   (212) 489-3994

MAYNARD, EDWARD
1. Barbados
2. Anthropology
3. Hostos Community College
   475 Grand Concourse
   Bronx, NY 10451
   (212) 960-1025

MERINO, ROLANDO
1. Dominican Republic
2. Public Health & Medical Sciences
3. Mt. Sinai School of Medicine
   1 Gustave L. Levy Place
   New York, NY 10029
   (212) 650-7836

MIRANDA, SYLVIA
1. Puerto Rico
2. History
3. Bronx Community College
   University Ave. & West 181st Street
   Bronx, NY 10453
   (212) 220-6050

MOSCOSO, FRANCISCO
1. Caribbean
2. History
3. Herbert H. Lehman College
   Bedford Park Blvd. West
   Bronx, NY 10468
   (212) 960-8281/8282

PACHON, HARRY
1. Dominican Republic
2. Public Administration &
   Political Science
3. Bernard M. Baruch College
   17 Lexington Ave.
   New York, NY 10010
   (212) 725-3375

PEPPE, PATRICK
1. Nicaragua
2. Political Science
3. Herbert H. Lehman College & GSUC
   Bedford Park Blvd. West
   Bronx, NY 10468
   (212) 960-8518

PIERCE, PAULETTE
1. Cuba
2. Sociology
3. Queens College
   65-30 Kissena Blvd.
   Flushing, NY 11367
   (718) 520-7088

PIÑEIRO, MARIA ELENA
1. Cuba
2. History
3. Hostos Community College
   475 Grand Concourse
   Bronx, NY 10451
   (212) 960-1075

PRIESTLEY, GEORGE
1. Central America
2. Political Science
3. Queens College
   65-30 Kissena Blvd.
   Flushing, NY 11367
   (718) 520-7334/7057

RICKETTS, EROL
1. Caribbean
2. Sociology
3. Graduate School
   33 West 42nd Street
   New York, NY 10036
   (212) 790-4386

RIOS, PALMIRA
1. Puerto Rico
2. Sociology
3. Herbert H. Lehman College
   Bedford Park Blvd. West
   Bronx, NY 10468
   (212) 960-8280

RIVERA, MARTA
1. Puerto Rico
2. Sociology
3. Hostos Community College
   475 Grand Concourse
   Bronx, NY 10451
   (212) 960-1066

ROMAN, PETER
1. Cuba
2. Political Science
3. Hostos Community College
   475 Grand Concourse
   Bronx, NY 10451
   (212) 960-1317/1066

ROSE, DAVID
1. English-speaking Caribbean
2. Medical Education,
   General Internal Medicine &
   Preventive Medicine
3. Mt. Sinai School of Medicine
   1 Gustave L. Levy Place
   New York, NY 10029
   (212) 650-7849

SAMAD-MATIAS, MARGARITA
1. Cuba, Central America
2. History
3. City College
   Convent Ave. & 138th Street
   New York, NY 10031
   (212) 690-8117/8118

SCHNEIDER, RONALD
1. Guatemala
2. Political Science
3. Queens College & GSUC
   65-30 Kissena Blvd.
   Flushing, NY 11367
   (718) 520-7402

SEARS, ALFRED
1. Caribbean
2. History & Political Science
3. Hunter College
   695 Park Ave.
   New York, NY 10021
   (212) 772-5035

SILVER, ALAN
1. English-speaking Caribbean
2. Medical Education,
   General Internal Medicine &
   Preventive Medicine
3. Mt. Sinai School of Medicine
   1 Gustave L. Levy Place
   New York, NY 10029
   (212) 650-7700

SINGHAM, ARCHIBALD
1. Caribbean
2. Political Science
3. Brooklyn College & GSUC
   Bedford Ave. & Ave. H
   Brooklyn, NY 11210
   (718) 780-5638

SU, VINCENT
1. Puerto Rico
2. Economics
3. Bernard M. Baruch College
   17 Lexington Ave.
   New York, NY 10010
   (212) 725-3066

SUSS, STUART
1. Caribbean
2. History
3. Kingsborough Community College
   2001 Oriental Blvd.
   Brooklyn, NY 11235
   (718) 935-5170

THOMAS, CUTHBERT
1. Caribbean
2. Political Science
3. Brooklyn College
   Bedford Ave. & Ave. H
   Brooklyn, NY 11210
   (718) 780-5350

VOURKAS, ARGYRIOS
1. Dominican Republic
2. Sociology
3. Queensborough Community
   College
   222-05 56th Ave.
   Bayside, NY 11364
   (718) 631-6255

WATERBURY, RONALD
1. Guatemala, Honduras
2. Anthropology
3. Queens College
   65-30 Kissena Blvd.
   Flushing, NY 11367
   (718) 520-7046

WHITE, RUSSELL
1. Central America
2. Geography
3. Hunter College
   695 Park Ave.
   New York, NY 10021
   (212) 772-5265

WOLF, ERIC
1. Central America
2. Anthropology
3. Herbert H. Lehman College & GSUC
   Bedford Park Blvd. West
   Bronx, NY 10468
   (212) 960-8518

ZAMBRANA, RAFÆL
1. Puerto Rico
2. Public Administration
3. Medgar Evers College
   1150 Carroll Street
   Brooklyn, NY 11225
   (718) 735-1971

3. South American Scholars

BESSE, SUSAN
1. Brazil
2. History
3. City College
   Convent Ave. & 138th Street
   New York, NY 10031
   (212) 690-5410

BONILLA, FRANK
1. Brazil, Venezuela
2. Sociology
3. Hunter College & GSUC
   695 Park Ave.
   New York, NY 10021
   (212) 772-5585

BOSCH, SAMUEL J.
1. Argentina, Colombia
2. International Community Medicine
3. Mt. Sinai School of Medicine
   1 Gustave L. Levy Place
   New York, NY 10029
   (212) 650-7941

BRAVEBOY-WAGNER, JAQUELINE
1. Guyana, Venezuela
2. Political Science
3. City College
   Convent Ave. & 138th Street
   New York, NY 10031
   (212) 690-5470

CHANG-RODRIGUEZ, EUGENIO
1. Peru
2. Latin American Studies
3. Queens College
   65-30 Kissena Blvd.
   Flushing, NY 11367
   (718) 520-7100

DeBŒR, WARREN
1. Peru, Bolivia
2. Anthropology
3. Queens College & GSUC
   65-30 Kissena Blvd.
   Flushing, NY 11367
   (718) 520-7364

DELLA CAVA, RALPH
1. Brazil
2. History
3. Queens College & GSUC
   65-30 Kissena Blvd.
   Flushing, NY 11367
   (718) 520-7364

DEUSCHLE, KURT W.
1. Colombia
2. International Community Medicine
3. Mt. Sinai School of Medicine
   1 Gustave L. Levy Place
   New York, NY 10029
   (212) 650-7831

EDEL, MATTHEW
1. Colombia, Brazil
2. Economics & Urban Studies
3. Queens College & GSUC
   65-30 Kissena Blvd.
   Flushing, NY 11367
   (718) 520-7530

ELIJOVICH, FERNANDO
1. Argentina
2. General Internal Medicine
3. Mt. Sinai School of Medicine
   1 Gustave L. Levy Place
   New York, NY 10029
   (212) 650-6778

ERICKSON, KENNETH
1. Brazil
2. Political Science
3. Hunter College & GSUC
   695 Park Ave.
   New York, NY 10021
   (212) 772-5498

FONT, MAURICIO
1. Brazil
2. Sociology
3. Queens College
   65-30 Kissena Blvd.
   Flushing, NY 11367
   (718) 520-7094

GERASSI, JOHN
1. South America
2. Political Science
3. Queens College
   65-30 Kissena Blvd.
   Flushing, NY 11367
   (718) 520-7373

GRANT, GERALDINE
1. Chile
2. Anthropology
3. LaGuardia Community College
   31-10 Thomson Ave.
   Long Island City, NY 11101
   (718) 626-5540

GRESSEL, DANIEL L.
1. Chile
2. Economics
3. Bernard M. Baruch College
   17 Lexington Ave.
   New York, NY 10010
   (212) 725-3009

GROSS, DANIEL
1. Brazil
2. Anthropology
3. Hunter College & GSUC
   695 Park Ave.
   New York, NY 10021
   (212) 570-5758

HANSEN, EDWARD
1. Brazil
2. Anthropology
3. Queens College & GSUC
   65-30 Kissena Blvd.
   Flushing, NY 11367
   (718) 520-7265

HAYTON, ROBERT
1. Argentina, Chile
2. Political Science & Law
3. Hunter College & GSUC
   695 Park Ave.
   New York, NY 10021
   (212) 772-5500

HEGEMAN, BETSY
1. Colombia
2. Anthropology
3. John Jay College
   444 West 56th Street
   New York, NY 10019
   (212) 489-3994

HELLMAN, RONALD G.
1. Chile, Colombia
2. Sociology & Political Science
3. Graduate School
   33 West 42nd Street
   New York, NY 10036
   (212) 382-2047

KINSBRUNER, JAY
1. Chile
2. History
3. Queens College & GSUC
   65-30 Kissena Blvd.
   Flushing, NY 11367
   (718) 520-7364

MERINO, ROLANDO
1. Chile
2. Public Health & Medical Sciences
3. Mt. Sinai School of Medicine
   1 Gustave L. Levy Place
   New York, NY 10029
   (212) 650-7836

NASH, JUNE
1. Bolivia
2. Anthropology
3. City College & GSUC
   Convent Ave. & 138th Street
   New York, NY 10031
   (212) 690-6608

PEPPE, PATRICK
1. Chile
2. Political Science
3. Herbert H. Lehman College
   & GSUC
   Berdford Park Blvd. West
   Bronx, NY 10468
   (212) 960-8518

PIERCE, PAULETTE
1. Guyana
2. Sociology
3. Queens College
   65-30 Kissena Blvd.
   Flushing, NY 11367
   (718) 520-7088

RANDALL, LAURA
1. Argentina, Brazil, Venezuela
2. Economics
3. Hunter College
   695 Park Ave.
   New York, NY 10021
   (212) 772-5400

RANIS, PETER
1. Argentina
2. Political Science
3. York College
   150-14 Jamaica Ave.
   Jamaica, NY 11451
   (718) 969-4363/4366

ROMAN, PETER
1. Chile
2. Political Science
3. Hostos Community College & GSUC
   475 Grand Concourse
   Bronx, NY 10451
   (212) 960-1317/1066

SAMAD-MATIAS, MARGARITA
1. Guyana, Surinam
2. History
3. City College
   Convent Ave. & 138th Street
   New York, NY 10031
   (212) 690-8117/8118

SCHNEIDER, RONALD
1. Brazil, Colombia
2. Political Science
3. Queens College
   65-30 Kissena Blvd.
   Flushing, NY 11367
   (718) 520-7402

SPALDING, HOBART
1. South America
2. History
3. Brooklyn College
   Bedford Ave. & Ave. H
   Brooklyn, NY 11210
   (718) 780-5198

SPIEGEL, HANS
1. Venezuela
2. Urban Studies
3. Hunter College
   695 Park Ave.
   New York, NY 10021
   (212) 772-5517

STINSON, SARA
1. Bolivia, Peru
2. Anthropology
3. Queens College & GSUC
   65-30 Kissena Blvd.
   Flushing, NY 11367
   (718) 520-7207

WATERBURY, RONALD
1. Ecuador
2. Anthropology
3. Queens College
   65-30 Kissena Blvd.
   Flushing, NY 11367
   (718) 520-7046

4. Latin American Scholars

BERGAD, LAIRD
1. Latin America
2. History
3. Herbert H. Lehman College
   Bedford Park Blvd. West
   Bronx, NY 10468
   (212) 960-8280

BINDLER, NORMAN
1. Latin America
2. History
3. Bronx Community College
   University Ave. & West 181st Street
   Bronx, NY 10453
   (212) 220-6315

CANTOR, PAUL
1. Latin America
2. Economics
3. Herbert H. Lehman College
   Bedford Park Blvd. West
   Bronx, NY 10468
   (212) 960-8297

DOLAN, EILEEN
1. Latin America
2. Community Nursing
3. Mt. Sinai School of Medicine
   1 Gustave L. Levy Place
   New York, NY 10029
   (212) 650-7941

EHRENPREIS, S. D.
1. U.S. Policy in Latin America
2. History
3. Bronx Community College
   University Ave. & West 181st Street
   Bronx, NY 10453
   (212) 220-6010

de GARCIA, MIGDALIA
DeJESUS TORRES
1. Latin America
2. Anthropology & Sociology
3. John Jay College
   444 West 56th Street
   New York, NY 10019
   (212) 489-5055

FREIDENBERG, JUDITH
1. Latin America & the Caribbean
2. Anthropology
3. Mt. Sinai School of Medicine
   1 Gustave L. Levy Place
   New York, NY 10029
   (212)- 650-7852/46

LAWSON, RONALD
1. Latin America
2. Urban Studies
3. Queens College
   65-30 Kissena Blvd.
   Flushing, NY 11367
   (718) 520-7614

LEGASTO, AUGUSTO
1. Latin America
2. Management
3. Bernard M. Baruch College
   17 Lexington Ave.
   New York, NY 10010
   (212) 725-7123

NEWLING, BRUCE
1. Latin American Economic
   Geography
2. Economics
3. City College
   Convent Ave. & 138th Street
   New York, NY 10031
   (212) 690-5403

ORTIZ, ALTAGRACIA
1. Latin America
2. History
3. John Jay College
   444 West 56th Street
   New York, NY 10019
   (212) 489-5034

PRINCE, HOWARD
1. Latin America
2. Anthropology & History
3. Manhattan Community College
   199 Chambers Street
   New York, NY 10007
   (212) 618-1378

RADOSH, RONALD
1. U.S. Policy in Latin America
2. History
3. Queensborough Community
   College
   222-05 56th Ave.
   Bayside, NY 11364
   (718) 631-6291

SCHLESINGER, ARTHUR M., Jr.
1. U.S. Policy in Latin America
2. History
3. Graduate School
   33 West 42nd Street
   New York, NY 10036
   (212) 790-4261

STONE, IRVING
1. Latin America
2. Economics
3. Bernard M. Baruch College
   17 Lexington Ave.
   New York, NY 10010
   (212) 725-3066

TABB, WILLIAM
1. Latin America
2. Economics
3. Queens College
   65-30 Kissena Blvd.
   Flushing, NY 11367
   (718) 520-7361

TRABOULAY, DAVID
1. Colonial Latin America
2. History
3. Staten Island College
   715 Ocean Terrace
   Staten Island, NY 10301
   (718) 390-7727

WIECZERZAK, JOSEPH
1. U.S. Policy in Latin America
2. History
3. Bronx Community College
   University Ave. & West 181st Street
   Bronx, NY 10453
   (212) 220-6102

NAME INDEX

Adelphi University
Latin American Studies Program 1

AFS International/Intercultural Programs, Inc. 32

Archibald S. Alexander Library
Rutgers, the State University of New Jersey 176

All Nations Women's League, Inc. (ANWL) 33

American Bar Association
Central American Goal VIII Committee and Inter-American Law Committee 34

American Friends Service Committee (AFSC) ARCH
World Hunger/Global Development Program 35

American Jewish Committee
International Relations Department/Department of South American Affairs 36
Blaustein Library 177

American Jewish Congress
Commission on International Affairs 37

The Americas Society 38

Americas Watch Committee 39

Amnesty International U.S. Section 40

Numbers refer to entries.

Anti-Defamation League of B'nai B'rith (ADL)
Department of Latin American Affairs 41

The Argentine-American Chamber of Commerce, Inc. 99

Argentine-North American Association for the Advancement of Science, Technology and Culture (ANACITEC) 42

The Association of the Bar of the City of New York
Committee on Inter-American Affairs 43

Astor, Lenox and Tilden Foundation Research Libraries
New York Public Library 194

Bernard M. Baruch College
Department of Black and Hispanic Studies 2

Bildner Center for Western Hemisphere Studies
Graduate School and University Center (CUNY) 12

Blaustein Library
American Jewish Committee 177

Elmer Holmes Bobst Library
New York University 178

Brazilian-American Chamber of Commerce, Inc. 100

Brooklyn College (CUNY)
Africana Studies 3
Area Studies 4
Caribbean Studies 5
Puerto Rican Studies 6

Campaign for Peace and Democracy/East and West 44

Care 45

Carnegie Corporation of New York 46

Carnegie Council on Ethics and International Affairs
(formerly: Council on Religion and International Affairs) 47

Numbers refer to entries.

Consulate General of the Republic of Trinidad and Tobago 138

Consulate General of St. Kitts and Nevis 139

Consulate General of Saint Lucia 140

Consulate General of St. Vincent and the Grenadines 141

Consulate General of Uruguay 142

Consulate General of Venezuela 143

Council of the Americas 57

Council on Foreign Relations 58

Council on Foreign Relations Library 182

Council on International and Public Affairs 59

Corporación de Fomento de la Producción
New York Office 104

Cuban National Planning Office (CNPC)
New York Office/National Office 60

Dominican Institute for Research and Social Action, Inc. 61

Duane Library
Fordham University 183

Ecuadorean Government Trade Office 105

Empire State College (SUNY)
Metropolitan New York Regional Center Bilingual Program 10

Federal Reserve Bank of New York 106

Raymond Fogelman Library
New School for Social Research 184

Ford Foundation 62

Numbers refer to entries.

Fordham University
Puerto Rican Studies Institute 11
Duane Library 183

Foreign Policy Association (FPA) 63

The Foundation Center 64

The Fund for Free Expression 65

The Fund for Peace 66

Governor's Office for Hispanic Affairs 107

Graduate School and University Center (CUNY)
Bildner Center for Western Hemisphere Studies 12
Mina Rees Library 199
Research Group on Socialism and Democracy 13

Hispanic Policy Development Project (HPDP) 67

The Hispanic Society of America 68

The Hispanic Society of America Library 185

The Hispanic Institute of the United States 14

Eugenio María de Hostos Community College (CUNY)
Latin American and Caribbean Studies 15

Hunter College (CUNY)
Center for Puerto Rican Studies 16
Latin American and Caribbean Studies Program 17
Jacqueline Wexler Library 202

Huntington Free Library,
Library of the Museum of the American Indian 186

Icarus Film 187

Institute of International Education (IIE) 69

Numbers refer to entries.

Numbers refer to entries.

New York University (Cont'd)
Graduate School of Business Administration Library 196
Museum Studies Program 25
School of Law Library 197

North American-Chilean Chamber of Commerce, Inc. 111

North American Congress on Latin America (NACLA) 86

Northeast Hispanic Catholic Center 87

Pace University
Institute of Brazilian-American Business 26
Pace University Library 198

Pan American Society 88

Parliamentarians Global Action 89

Permanent Mission of Argentina to the United Nations 144

Permanent Mission of the Bahamas to the United Nations 145

Permanent Mission of Barbados to the United Nations 146

Permanent Mission of Belize to the United Nations 147

Permanent Mission of Bolivia to the United Nations 148

Permanent Mission of Brazil to the United Nations 149

Permanent Mission of Chile to the United Nations 150

Permanent Mission of Colombia to the United Nations 151

**Permanent Mission of the Commonwealth of Dominica
to the United Nations** 152

Permanent Mission of Costa Rica to the United Nations 153

Permanent Mission of Cuba to the United Nations 154

Numbers refer to entries.

Numbers refer to entries.

Permanent Mission of Uruguay to the United Nations 174

Permanent Mission of Venezuela to the United Nations 175

Peru-Commercial Office 112

The Population Council 90

Port Authority of New York and New Jersey 113

Puerto Rico Chamber of Commerce in the U.S., Inc. 114

Queens College (CUNY)
Latin American Area Studies 27
Paul Klapper Library 188

Mina Rees Library
The Graduate School & University Center (CUNY) 199

Research Institute for the Study of Man 91

Rutgers, the State University of New Jersey
Latin American Studies Program 28
Department of Puerto Rican and Hispanic Caribbean Studies 29

The Schomburg Center for Research in Black Culture
New York Public Library 195

Seton Hall University
McLaughlin Library 191

Social Science Research Council 92

Spanish Institute 93

Harry A. Sprague Library
Montclair State College 200

State University of New York at Stony Brook
Department of History 30

The Tinker Foundation Incorporated 94

Numbers refer to entries.

Numbers refer to entries.

SUBJECT INDEX

Numbers refer to entries.